MOTI MAHAL'S
Tandoori Trail

OTHER TITLES

Continental Cuisine for the Indian Palate
Street Foods of India
The Indian Vegetarian Cookbook
The Landour Cookbook
Art of Indian Cuisine
Traditional Kashmiri Cuisine: Wazwaan

CHEFS' SPECIAL SERIES

Bengali Kitchen
Chinese Kitchen
Kashmiri Kitchen
Favourite Indian Desserts
Low Calorie Desserts
Nepalese Kitchen
Punjabi Kitchen
Rajasthani Kitchen
South Indian Kitchen
Goan Kitchen
Parsi Kitchen
Kerala Kitchen
Marwari Kitchen
Gujarati Kitchen
Delhi Kitchen
Vegetarian Fiesta

MOTI MAHAL'S
Tandoori Trail

Monish Gujral

Lustre Press
Roli Books

Roli Books Pvt. Ltd.
Lustre Press Pvt. Ltd.
M-75 Greater Kailash II (Market)
New Delhi 110 048, India
Ph: ++91 (11) 2921 2271, 2921 2782, 2921 0886
Fax: ++91 (11) 2921 7185, E-mail: roli@vsnl.com
Website: rolibooks.com

Editor: Neeta Datta
Design: Sneha Pamneja

ISBN: 81-7436-316-5

Printed and bound by Thomson Press (India) Ltd.

To my father,
Nand Lal Gujral

Acknowledgements

How does one begin when there are so many people to thank?
Yet, the people most directly responsible for this book include my
wife, Sonal, without whom I would be lost.
To my mother, Rupa, who has been the backbone of my life;
My children, Tanisha and Gunav for being such perfect
and patient kids;
Ritu Dhawan for lending a sisterly hand whenever in need and
introducing me to the writing world;
My publisher, Pramod Kapoor, for believing in my
work and giving it life;
Sourish Bhattacharya, of *HT City*, for providing me with an
opportunity to write my recipe column in the *HT City*, which became
the basis to write this cookbook;
And Uma Vasudev for writing the introduction of this book.
Last but not least, to all Moti Mahal fans who swear by our butter
chicken and who have made Moti Mahal a household name.

Contents

Four generations of the Gujrals: Kundan Lal Gujral with his wife, Prakash Devi, holding their grandson, Monish. Standing next to Prakash Devi is daughter-in-law, Rupa; and Kundan Lal's mother, Maya Devi.

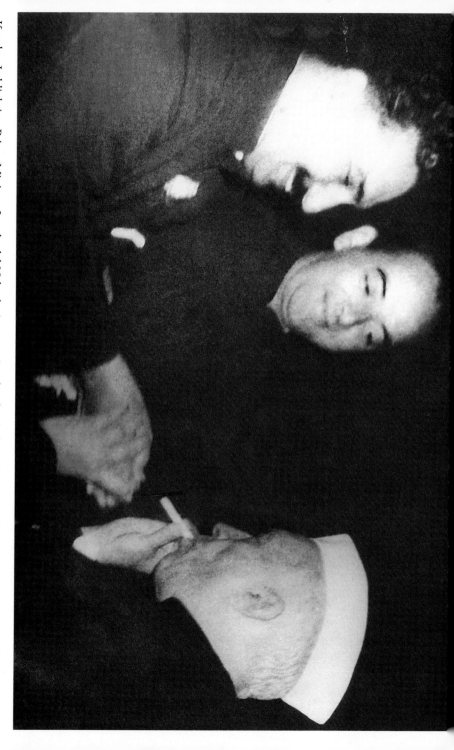

Kundan Lal lighting Prime Minister Jawaharlal Nehru's cigarette. Panditji banked on Moti Mahal's fare for most of the official meals, a tradition continued by his daughter, Indira Gandhi, when she became prime minister of India.

A Legend and the Man

This is the story of a man who set out on a culinary adventure and changed the face of Indian cooking.

This is the story of a man and a recipe which internationalized the Indian taste for succulence and spice in its food.

This is also the story of a man who made the curry a butter-filled delight, bringing to the ordinary chicken a special flavour. A man who turned the plebian village tandoor for baking into a royal mode for his innovation:

The tandoori chicken.

Then came the butter chicken.

The result: a revolution in taste, a change in Indian eating habits, and a place on the international gourmet map.

The man was Kundan Lal Gujral.

The restaurant where he housed his innovations was Moti Mahal. The two became a legendary mix.

The Partition of India in 1947 was followed by the Punjabi invasion of Delhi. The laid-back Dilliwallas, as the inhabitants of India's capital are called, were themselves a victim of the traumatizing effect of the changing post-Partition social equations. They did not have time to re-learn their priorities. If the Dilliwala felt paralyzed by the tragedy, the refugee-Punjabi was galvanized into fighting for a new avatar or rebirth. Lahore, the then capital of the united Punjab, was known as the Paris of the East for its music, art, theatre, and literary initiatives, even as the forerunner of Bollywood's later happening era. Those who fled from there, came to Delhi, rolled up their sleeves and putting cultural concerns onto the back burner, decided to first regain their economic dignity. Businessmen of standing, lawyers of repute, women reared in opulent luxury having lost all, decided to make their economic renewal a challenging venture. The Dilliwala was swamped by this aggressive desire of the Punjabi to rebuild. Millionaires, having lost everything, even took to selling wares on wayside trollies, women who had lifted a finger only to summon their maids took up jobs, creating the first post-Independence wave of the feminist assertion. All the horrific happenings of the Partition, rape, murder, loot, the reversal of fortunes, did not yet throw up a post-Partition Punjabi beggar on the street.

One of this intrepid breed to whom defeat was a dirty word was Kundan Lal Gujral. He was a Punjabi-Pathan from the North-West Frontier Province. This area, in what later became part of West Pakistan, comprised a unique blend of not only Hindu-Muslim culture but also a Punjabi-Pathan mix. The area was uniquely free of communal tension till the politics of Partition began to orchestrate the raucous theme of mutual hatred and the Hindu minority was constrained to flee across the newly created borders and vice-versa. Though his father, Dewan Chand, owned a cloth shop in Chakwal, a small town in district Jhelum, the young Kundan became a professional product of the capital city, Peshawar, where he got his first job. He was not even in his teens when he found himself in a position where he could exploit his own resources. He began to work as an assistant in an eatery and catering joint in 1920 owned by a sardar named Mukha Singh who took the youngster under his wing. In 1927, the eatery graduated into a restaurant and Peshawar became culinary home to the first Moti Mahal.

Rabindra Seth, well known columnist on tourism who himself hails from Peshawar and is one of the few who can regale history-hungry writers for memories of that era, recalls, 'The Moti Mahal of that period in Peshawar was more a takeaway joint. The tandoori rotis and kebabs were strung on skewers and cooked in the tandoor and constituted popular fare.'

Within three months, Kundan Lal's energetic salesmanship helped the eatery break even. He carved out such a personal niche for himself amongst the customers that he would serve that he soon established a warm rapport with the local gentry during eight years of his diligent apprenticeship.

Sardar Trilochan Singh, a Sikh Pathan also from Peshawar and now settled in Delhi, remembers Kundan Lal's early foray into the culinary world from his Peshawar days. 'He was a sturdy worker. He exuded this tremendous energy and enthusiasm in carrying out orders and reaching out to people. He was always on the move, establishing a clientele with an eager response to home deliveries.'

This honed Kundan Lal's skills in what he later described as the six P's for success—the quality of the Product, its Price, its Promotion, the Place, of course, and finally, the People, and Personalized service. Except for the Place which was lost to Partition, he came to Delhi armed with the other five guidelines and twelve thousand rupees which was all he could salvage from a tragedy that had robbed people not only of their possessions but also for many cases their entire families.

In 1947, both Mukha Singh and the thirty-seven-year-old Kundan Lal, with his wife Prakash Devi, son Nand, and widowed mother Maya Devi came to Delhi together as refugees. 'Mukha Singh went off to Dehradun and was never heard of again,' recalls Seth, 'while Kundan Lal stayed on in Delhi. He changed the face of Indian cookery.' Catering was his first love. It was to be his last and the most fruitful one. The trail which began in Gora Bazaar in Peshawar ended in Delhi's then liveliest intersection between the old city and the new—Daryaganj. There in 1947, Kundan Lal, by now on his own, identified a small *thara,* a little platform for a wayside café to which he decided to give its original name from across the Frontier.

Moti Mahal—The Palace of Pearls.

The pearls not to adorn the beauteous women of Delhi but to win the Dilliwala's gastronomic heart and give the world a new delight—the tandoori chicken. It was to spell culinary magic.

He had the chicken roasted in a mud-baked oven made from a hole dug into the ground and lit with wood or coal—the tandoor (derived from a Persian word). Along with this came the usual tandoori roti, constituting a thick ball of kneaded wheat, freshly baked in the same oven, made of the familiar ground wheat, but swollen to a crisp roundness. The combination was lethal for the weighty who were hard put to refrain and paradisiacal for those who could afford to splurge. When Kundan Lal added to this a vegetarian speciality—the *dal makhani* (black lentil cooked slowly overnight and mixed with tomato purée and topped with fresh cream)—even gourmets would visit Moti Mahal with mouth-watering expectancy. Gradually, Kundan Lal, with his lambswool cap, his thickly twirling moustache, his Pathani suit or sometimes trousers, tie and coat, his welcoming grace in following the traditional Indian custom of bending low to greet his older customers gave added flavour to the 'Moti Mahal Experience'.

Like each area of India which has its own distinct cuisine, the Dilliwala had his or her preferences for hot spicy snacks, fluffy round fried puris made of a mix of wholewheat flour and refined flour, vegetarian specialities, Mughlai meat, and chicken kormas or curry. The cylindrical mud-baked oven of two and a half feet, sometimes even above the ground, was typical of the northern Indian countryside where it formed a *sanjha-chulla*, the common oven, for the village women to bake their rotis. They would flatten a roti by tossing it from one palm of the hand to another and then clamp it on the side of the tandoor where the simmering firewood at the bottom would bake it to a golden brown. The oven can accommodate six or seven rotis at a time. There is a secondary hole through which air can be regulated. In the Frontier too it was used mainly to bake the rotis made of wholewheat or the naans made of refined flour. It is essentially a rural innovation which acquired a five-star hotel status via innovators like Kundan Lal. He was the first to come up with the idea that a whole chicken could also be cooked inside the tandoor. The result was phenomenal.

James Traub, the author of *India, the Challenge of Change* on a visit to India in 1984, described the tandoori chicken with typical gourmet flourish, 'It emerges, in the best of all possible restaurants, light pink in the centre, crisp on the outside, slightly smoky throughout and with a fine mist of sauce still clinging to the surface. It is pungent with cumin and coriander, rather than hot with chilli. One should give in, after the first bite of *murgh malai* or tender chicken, to the sudden desire to weep; India is an emotional country, after all.'

Kundan Lal was not the one to rest on his laurels. He came up shortly with another innovation that had people flocking to experience his gradually expanding empire of taste. He created the tandoori butter chicken, a succulent twin to the royal tandoori. And after introducing the innovative trend-setting *dal makhani*, the cream-bathed black lentil, he sat back and let the customers take over.

Camaraderie was established with his clientele in unforeseen ways. In the Fifties, in what was still a shack-like arrangement but which had the distinctive aroma of tandoori cooking wafting across to them, Inder Gujral, later to become India's prime minister, visited the restaurant one day with his brother Satish Gujral, the painter. He heard one of the waiters calling out frantically in Punjabi, 'Gujral sahib *da* phone, Gujral Sahib *da* phone!' Dressed in typical Pathani salwar-kameez, which was mandatory dress for the staff, the waiter was again a Peshawari from Punjab stock. Inder Gujral half got up to go to the phone when they realized that the call was for Kundan Lal Gujral, the proprietor who also happened to be a Gujral. Though the former's family was from the district of Jhelum in the province of Punjab that had gone into Pakistan territory, Kundan Lal came from another district which fell into the adjoining territory. While the other Gujrals remained in Jhelum and came to Delhi only when the Partition of India forced populations to migrate, a ten-year-old Kundan Lal had gone off to Peshawar in search of fortune as it were in the fulfillment of his catering dream. Twenty-seven years later, having made a name for himself, he had landed in Delhi to start afresh. He had come armed with Oscar Wilde's famous aphorism, 'to declare nothing but my genius'.

The first thing he did after setting up the little *thara* was to put into practice one of the six P's of his formula for success—public relations. In Peshawar one home that he would cater to regularly which was just a stone's throw away from their eatery was that of Mehr Chand Khanna, a political stalwart who became their patron. The same Mehr Chand Khanna later became a minister in the cabinet of India's first prime minister, Jawaharlal Nehru. In Delhi, instead of the tandoori kebabs and naans, Kundan Lal packed his innovative tandoori chicken for his mentor. The response was an urgent summon. Khanna wanted Kundan Lal's creation to be the main dish for a dinner he was hosting for the prime minister. At the dinner, Khanna coolly waited for the chicken to speak. And how! Nehru asked who the inventor was. Khanna produced Kundan Lal. Thereafter the Moti Mahal speciality became a must in Nehru's banquets, dinners and meals for political meets. It was possibly a Kundan Lal recipe which provoked the famous remark attributed to Nehru when he saw some junior colleagues biting into the succulent pieces of chicken at a lunch with frenzied zest: 'Easy, easy, my friend, the chicken has been cooked. It's not going to run away!' Indira Gandhi continued the practice of banking on Moti Mahal fare for official meals when she herself became the prime minister. Before that, as Inder Malhotra, famous journalist and author recalls, he and Feroze Gandhi were regulars at the Moti Mahal restaurant itself and occasionally Indira Gandhi would be seen there as well.

'We voted for Moti Mahal with our feet and mouth,' says Malhotra. 'Whenever the occasion arose for eating out, we would automatically head for Moti Mahal. Feroze would have a sample of the chicken dishes but the *dal makhani* was his special favourite. I loved the tandoori chicken. Though Kundan Lal was always customer friendly, the fact that Feroze was Pandit Nehru's son-in-law got us even more attention.'

Kundan Lal, like everybody in those heady post-Independence years, was a great admirer of Jawaharlal Nehru, the acknowledged architect of modern India. Though the cuisine had reached the prime minister's house, Kundan Lal's persistent desire was to meet his idol personally. There was one person from the old days in Peshawar who could do it—Mohammad Yunus, the then chief of protocol, but whose political affiliations stretched back to the pre-Independence struggle in the North-West Frontier Province as a Pathan and political secretary of Khan Abdul Ghaffar Khan, who was known as Frontier Gandhi. Yunus chose to opt for India after Partition, joined the Indian Foreign Service and remained a close confidante of Nehru. He too was a frequent visitor at Moti Mahal. 'Khan,' said Kundan Lal to him one day, 'there is one thing you must do for me, take me to Panditji.' Yunus did that and in the typically Indian gesture of paying respect Kundan Lal bent low to touch his feet when he saw Nehru.

Thereafter, Moti Mahal became the first venue for local and visiting dignitaries to sample this most innovative and popular Indian cuisine. Not only did the list of Moti Mahal faithfuls read like the who's who of India but gradually of visiting presidents and prime ministers of other countries. It was India's education minister, Maulana Azad, who said to the Shah of Iran, when he was on a state visit to India that coming to Delhi without eating at Moti Mahal would be like visiting Agra without seeing the Taj, or New York without seeing the Statue of Liberty! The list went on to include the late US President Richard Nixon, the then Canadian Prime Minister Pierre Trudeau, the King of Nepal, and Soviet leaders Alexie Kosygin, Nikolai Bulganin, and Nikita Krushchev. The latter was so impressed with the Kundan invention that he asked him to open a branch of his restaurant at an international trade fair in Moscow. Nearer home Pakistan's Zulfikar Ali Bhutto, a known gourmet, became a regular at Moti Mahal whenever in India, while India's Field Marshall Sam Maneckshaw who led India to victory in the Bangladesh war was an equal enthusiast. Kundan Lal's own satisfaction knew no bounds when, having started off by winning the taste buds of his own country's prime minister, he went on to win those of the next generation and the next…. It was Moti Mahal's specialities which dominated the menu for the wedding dinner of Jawaharlal Nehru's grandson, Sanjay.

Imitation they say is the best form of flattery. The tandoori chicken, the butter chicken, *dal makhani*, tandoori roti, and naan became staple fare in almost all restaurants serving Indian food. While hotel restaurants came in later as strong rivals, fast food joints have sabotaged the leisured pace at which good food can be enjoyed. But the Moti Mahal flavour has continued to hold its secret passport to gourmet country as no other. Only two years ago, Robin Cook, the then British foreign secretary, declared that with an added flavour of sauce added to chicken *tikka* to lure the British palate, the chicken *tikka* masala has become Britain's 'true national dish'. He was obviously not familiar with its real parentage, for what he was talking about was only the illegitimate offspring of the butter chicken created by Kundan Lal in its home country 50 years back.

As early as in 1947, Kundan Lal, ever receptive to yet another of his six P's for success, Promotion, introduced the popular form of music, *qwalli*, as the staple music for Moti Mahal loyalists. 'I remember hearing Shakila Banu the first time at the Daryaganj Moti Mahal in the early Seventies,' recalls Vasant Sathe, former minister for information and broadcasting in the government of India. 'At that time I made trips to Delhi to argue cases at the Supreme Court. After eating at Moti Mahal once with another lawyer friend of mine, we decided that each visit to Delhi would have to include at least one meal at Moti Mahal. What could be better than for food to sing its way into the stomach!'

That became the ultimate epitaph.

Prime Minister Jawaharlal Nehru chats with Mrs Kennedy in the Ashoka Room of the Rastrapati Bhavan before the luncheon (catered by Moti Mahal) hosted in her honour by the president of India.

Kundan Lal Gujral sharing a joke with Indira Gandhi celebrating one of her victories.

It won Kundan Lal a coveted place in the area of his expertise. In 1985-1986, he won the Gold Medal for introducing tandoori cuisine to the world in the Trans Himalayan Selection Award.

Then came the Worldwide Tourism Promotion Award in1987, a Gold Medal for tourist promotion in the restaurant category.

In 1991, he got the Indian Association of Tour Operators Hall of Fame Award.

In 1995, he won the Himalayan Hotel and Food Service Award in recognition of his innovation, the tandoori chicken, and his lifetime contribution to the hospitality industry.

But Kundan Lal was a rarity. Success brought humility and the urge to give back to society what he had earned from it. There would be occasions which would remind him of his own days of need. He once saw a frail old man plying a trolley on the road as he was driving past in his chauffeur-driven car. The trolley was heavy with a mound of *gur* (jaggery), which the man was too weak to push. Kundan Lal stopped the car and bought the whole mound.

'He retained all the old world values,' recalls Dolly Arora, Kundan Lal's *rakhi* sister. 'All my success lies at my mother's feet,' she quoted him as saying as he would bend in reverence to her the first thing every morning. Then he would do his puja, water the sacred *tulsi* plant and offer his obeisance to the sun. Late every night, after closing the restaurant, he would go to Gurdwara Sisganj to pay homage to the Sikh gurus. The family had both, a Hindu puja room in the house as well as a room for the *Guru Granth Sahib*, the sacred book of the Sikhs.

He also made it a practice, when on his visit to the gurdwara, to distribute blankets to the poor. He would also be readily available during the day for those who sought his growing influence to have their work done. He was always ready to cajole his influential friends to help his needy ones. 'There came a time,' recalls Bhajan Lal Chauhan, an old friend, 'when there would be a queue of people waiting at his house to hand him petitions!' At one point he was even appointed juror, but he fought shy of politics. He preferred to be in his restaurant amidst the aromas of his culinary inventions, the chatter of friends and the rumbustious beats of the *qwalli* which would punctuate the air with its rhythmic assertions. He loved to hear the typical Indian exclamation of ecstatic admiration, the '*wah, wahs*' that would greet the singer. He loved the area behind his beloved restaurant, Kucha Challan, in the heart of Delhi, where he stayed for years after Partition. 'But the growing needs of the younger generation of his family,' recalls Rupa Gujral, his daughter-in-law, 'finally took him to an opulent house in the aristocratic area of old Delhi on Rajpur road.' He died there in 1997, surrounded by opulence, but with a heart as nostalgic as ever for the area and atmosphere symbolized by his restaurant, where the simplicity of décor was like an added spice and not a subtraction, from the rich, succulent, luxuriating aromas of his culinary success.

'My restaurant is my life,' said Kundan Lal towards the end of his great innings. It is to Kundan Lal's innovative genius that we can attribute the popular place that tandoori cuisine has acquired in Indian cookery. It became a lesson well learnt for the family left behind, in particular, for his grandsons trained in hotel management. Monish Gujral, the younger one, having had the opportunity to learn special recipes from his grandfather, writes a food column, but is raring to conquer the international palate in its home ground. To commemorate Kundan Lal's tandoori trail from Peshawar to Delhi, Monish launched the upmarket Moti Mahal Delux: Tandoori Trail restaurants. He was inspired also by his late father, Nand Lal, who died before he could translate his dream into reality. Monish has taken up the challenge. He now plans to take this succulent trail across the globe. This would be a tribute, he says, to his grandfather.

Perhaps the new nomenclature in the menu for the tandoori chicken, to do full justice to his grandfather's innovative genius could be, 'Kundan chicken—tandoori style!'

— Uma Vasudev

Herbs Spices and Other Ingredients

Aniseed (saunf): Yellowish green seeds similar to cumin seeds. They have a sweet taste and are used to flavour certain dishes and are chewed after meals as they help in digestion. Aniseed has a cooling effect on our body and has high digestive qualities. It also has medicinal properties as it is good for the stomach and liver.

Asafoetida (hing): A pale yellow spice with a very strong and distinct flavour. It is used in small quantities to enhance the flavour of the dish. It is high in minerals especially in calcium and iron. Good asafoetida will dissolve completely in water. Indian physicians like Charak and Bhattacharya describe the uses of this condiment as medicinal.

Bay leaf (tej patta): These fragrant leaves are used in dried form. They are used in curries and rice preparations.

Black pepper (kali mirch): Freshly ground black pepper used in Indian cooking adds to the flavour of the dish.

Cardamom (elaichi): This spice is native to India and is considered to be most prized after saffron. Cardamom pods can be used with or without their husks and have a slightly pungent and aromatic taste. Cardamom pods come in a variety of colours: green, white, and black. The green and white pods can be used in both savoury and sweet dishes, but the black ones are mainly used in savoury dishes.

Carom seeds (ajwain): These are dark brownish small seeds, which look like celery seeds and are slightly pungent. They give an aromatic flavour to the dish.

Chilli powder: A very fiery spice to be used with precaution. There are various brands in the market and the heat varies from brand to brand. You can adjust the quantity to suit your taste. *Degi Mirch* powder (paprika) may be used to enhance the colour of the dish.

Chillies, red, dried (sookhi lal mirch): These pods are whole or dried, they are extremely fiery, so caution may be exercised in their use. To make them milder, you can gently remove the seeds. Dried chillies are usually fried in oil before use.

Cinnamon (dalchini): It has a delicate, sweet aroma. Cinnamon comes from the bark of tree. It is sold both in powdered and flattish stick form. It has been used since Biblical times—first in combination with other ingredients as a body scent. It is used for flavouring purposes—in pickles and pies. Cinnamon has a warming effect and is to be used in small quantity. It is good for colds and digestion.

Cloves (laung): These buds have a sharp, pungent, piquant, and bitter taste. They are used to flavour savory and sweet dishes. Cloves have an aphrodisiac effect. They also have a warming effect and are used in hot teas, soups, preserves, pulaos, etc.

Coriander (dhaniya) seeds: Coriander seeds are ground to a fine powder. They are used extensively in Indian cooking to thicken curries. Ground coriander is an aromatic powder, has a cooling effect and is good for digestion. It is high in potassium, phosphorus, calcium, iron, and vitamins A and B.

Coriander leaves (hara dhaniya), fresh: It is a fragrant herb used as an ingredient as well as a garnish. It has a cooling effect on the body and makes the food digestible. Coriander leaves are also known as cilantro or Chinese parsley.

Cumin (jeera) seeds: These are pale brown oval seeds, used extensively in Indian cooking. These seeds have a musty smell and a strong aroma and can be used whole or in a powdered form. Cumin seeds are widely used in flavouring lentils and vegetables. They have volatile oil—thymine (3-5%) which is responsible for their taste and flavour. As a condiment, cumin seeds are very rich in iron, calcium, potassium, phosphorus, and also sodium and are good for the liver, eyes, and stomach.

Cumin seeds, black (shah jeera): These are fine, slender seeds a little darker in colour. They are used for flavouring curries and rice.

Curry leaves (kadhi patta): They are available fresh or dried and are used for flavouring lentils and vegetables. Most Indian homes grow this plant in a pot so as to obtain fresh curry leaves.

Fenugreek seeds (methi dana): These are dried, flat yellow seeds and have an aromatic bitter taste, which improves when lightly fried. These seeds are very hard and can be ground. In their powdered form they constitute an important ingredient in Indian curries, powders, and pastes. Fenugreek seeds also have medicinal values. They have a cooling effect. Fenugreek leaves are extremely rich in iron, calcium, sulphur, chlorine, vitamins A and C. They are good for digestion and help sluggish liver and lungs. High sulphur and chlorine give these leaves a cleansing effect. The seeds are rich in phosphorus and potassium as well as organic iron and calcium.

Garam masala: This is a mixture of spices, which can also be made at home besides being readily available in many Indian supermarkets. There is no exact formula, but a typical mixture may include black cumin seeds, black peppercorns, cloves, cinnamon, and black cardamom. Proportions may be as follows: 1 cinnamon 2½ cm stick, 3 cloves, 3 black peppercorns, 2 black cardamom, 2½ tsp black cumin seeds all ground in a grinder.

Garlic (lasan): Garlic is a standard ingredient mostly used as pastes in most Indian dishes. Bottled garlic paste is now readily available in stores. Garlic affects our body chemistry in two distinct ways. It has been established by research that it lowers blood cholesterol, improves HDL \ LDL ratio, improves blood circulation, prevents blood clotting and reduces the body's production of fats. The second effect is antiseptic, antibiotic, and antifungal.

Ghee: It is a cooking medium. There are two types of ghee: pure (a dairy product) and vegetable. Earlier it was a matter of pride to use pure (desi) ghee as cooking medium, but in modern days studies showed that pure ghee is high in cholesterol, so vegetable oil was readily accepted as a safe cooking medium. To make desi ghee at home take 250 gm of butter, melt in a heavy-bottomed saucepan and let it simmer for 10-12 minutes. Once the white froth becomes golden in colour, remove from heat and strain through a muslin cloth.

Ginger (adrak): It is one of the most important ingredients used in Indian kitchens. Bottled ginger paste is also available in stores. 2½ cm ginger is equal to 1 tsp of ginger paste. Ginger has gingerin and potassium oxalate in large quantities. Fresh ginger has some effective volatile oils, which are not present in dried ginger (*sonth*). Fibrous ginger has some medicinal qualities. Ginger is an anti-coagulant and it stimulates the heart.

Gram flour (besan): It is made from lentils. Gram flour is used as a binding agent.

Mace (javitri): This is a lacy covering of a seed of the nutmeg tree. Indians use it sparingly adding it to only rich creamy dishes. It is mostly added to various spice blends. It has a rich, warm aroma and a sweet flavour.

Mango powder (amchur): It is made from dried, raw mango (sun dried) and ground to a fine powder. It is sour to taste. It is used in preparation of various drinks, spice blends, and chutneys.

Melon seeds (magaz): These are shelled seeds of melon used to make curries thick and rich. Melon seeds have a sweet flavour. They are also added to drinks and desserts.

Mint (pudina): A fragrant green herb. It is used in fresh form in *raitas*, *lassis* or to make chutneys. It is also added to biryani (a rice dish). It is very high in vitamins A, B and C as also in calcium, iron, phosphorus, sulphur, and chlorine. Sulphur and chlorine give it cleansing properties. It is good for digestion and for the liver and hardened arteries.

Mustard seeds (rai): These are small round seeds, yellow or reddish brown in colour. Dark seeds are pungent and mostly used in curries and pickles.

Nutmeg (jaiphal): It is a lacy covering on a nutmeg kernel. It has a rich warm fragrance and sweet flavour. Used as spice blend.

Onion seeds (kalonji): These triangular seeds are black in colour. They are used in curries and to make pickles.

Pomegranate seeds (anar dana): These are sun-dried seeds of sour pomegranate. These seeds have a sour taste and a subtle sweetness. They are available as whole and in powdered form and are used in chutneys and various tangy dishes.

Poppy seeds (khus khus): Although they are from opium poppy they do not contain opium. They are dried, whole whitish seeds. They are used in certain Indian curries.

Rose water (gulab jal): A distilled liquid from rose petals used for flavouring sweet dishes.

Saffron (kesar): It is available in strands and has a lovely aroma. It is made from stigmas of the saffron crocus. Saffron is used to colour and flavour the dish. Soak the strands in a little warm water or milk and then add to the dish. It is used as a condiment for its aroma, flavour, and cooling effect. Ayurveda uses it for lot of medicine preparation. It is a good stimulant for the liver, brain, spleen, and a general tonic.

Sesame seeds (til): They are whole, flat, cream-coloured seeds used to flavour curries.

Tamarind (imli): The dried pods of tamarind or Indian date are sour to taste and very sticky. Tamarind has to be soaked in water and strained before use. Tamarind paste is available in supermarkets.

Turmeric (haldi) powder: This is a yellowish bitter tasting spice, which is sold in powder form. It is used to give colour to the dish. Turmeric has medicinal properties. It is good for stomach problems, heals internal wounds, and is an antiseptic.

Vetivier essence (kewda): It is an essence of screwpine and is used to flavour sweet dishes and rice.

Basic Recipes

Although, now most of the spices are available in the food stores all over the world, it is imperative that some of the important ones to be made in home for fresh aromatic spices to flavour your dishes.

Tandoori Masala

Take 2 tbsp / 12 gm cumin (*jeera*) seeds, 2 tbsp / 12 gm coriander (*dhaniya*) seeds, 1 tbsp black peppercorns (*sabut kali mirch*), 1 tbsp cloves (*laung*), ½ tsp red chilli powder, and ½ tsp black salt.

In a non-stick pan, roast the cumin seeds, coriander seeds, black peppercorns, and cloves over medium heat for about a minute until a pleasant aroma emanates. Remove from heat and keep aside to cool. Grind to a fine powder add the remaining ingredients and mix well. Store in an airtight jar.

Garam Masala

Take 15 black cardamom (*badi elaichi*) pods, seeds only, 3 tbsp cloves (*laung*), 2 tbsp black peppercorns (*sabut kali mirch*), 2 tbsp / 12 gm cumin (*jeera*) seeds, 1 mace (*javitri*), 5 cinnamon (*dalchini*) sticks, 1" each, 1 nutmeg (*jaiphal*), 5 green cardamom (*choti elaichi*) pods, seeds only, 2 tsp / 5 gm ginger powder (*sonth*), and a few strands of saffron (*kesar*).

Roast all the ingredients in a non-stick pan over medium heat till a fragrant smell emanates. Remove the pan from the heat and grind in a spice grinder to a fine powder. Store in an airtight jar.

Chaat Masala

Take 1 tsp / 1½ gm carom (*ajwain*) seeds, 3 tbsp / 18 gm cumin (*jeera*) seeds, 1 tbsp / 18 gm ginger (*adrak*), ground, 2 tsp / 4 gm mango powder (*amchur*), 2 tbsp black salt, 1 tsp / 4 gm salt, 1 tsp / 2 gm black pepper (*kali mirch*) powder, and ½ tsp red chilli powder.

Roast the carom and cumin seeds in a non-stick pan. Grind all the ingredients in a spice grinder to a fine powder and store in an airtight jar.

Cottage Cheese (*paneer*)

A type of fresh cheese prepared by curdling milk, and then separating the curd from the whey by passing through a thin muslin cloth. The cheese remains in the cloth while the whey flows out. One should use full-cream milk for softer cottage cheese. Low-fat milk should be avoided as it yields tough and rubbery cottage cheese.

To prepare 250 gm cottage cheese: take 5 cups / 1 lt milk, 1 cup / 200 gm non-fat yoghurt (*dahi*), a piece of muslin cloth (2 feet long).

Take a large, heavy-bottomed saucepan; pour the milk and bring to the boil, stirring continuously to prevent skin forming on the top. As the milk comes to the boil, add yoghurt immediately. Keep stirring gently till the milk curdles and greenish whey separates. Remove from heat and let it cool for about 10 minutes. After a firm curd is formed, strain the mixture through a muslin cloth placed over a large, deep bowl. Tie the four ends of the cloth and hang it till the whey is strained through. The cottage cheese is collected in the cloth. If cubes of cottage cheese are desired then press the muslin cloth between two flat plates and place a heavy object over it for about 15 minutes. Remove and cut into the desired shape and size.

One can substitute Ricotta cheese for cottage cheese. It can be baked in the oven on high heat for about 35 minutes till the water dries up and can be cut into desired shape.

Vegetable Gravy

Take 1 kg onions, peeled, chopped; ½ cup / 100 gm ghee, 2 black cardamom (*moti elaichi*), 5 green cardamom (*choti elaichi*), 5 cloves (*laung*), 1 nutmeg (*jaiphal*), 2 gm mace (*javitri*), 5 gm cinnamon (*dalchini*) sticks, 2 bay leaves (*tej patta*), 2 tbsp / 36 gm ginger-garlic (*lasan-adrak*) paste, 2½ cups / 200 gm cashew nuts (*kaju*), 100 gm melon seeds (*magaz*), 2½ cups / 500 ml milk, ½ cup / 100 gm tomato purée, 1½ tsp / 3 gm salt, 2 tsp / 4 gm red chilli powder, 1½ tsp / 3 gm garam masala, 1 tsp / 2 gm white pepper (*safed mirch*) powder, and ½ cup / 100 gm yoghurt (*dahi*).

Method:

○ Boil the onions with 2½ cups water. Then simmer for about 25 minutes on low heat. Drain the water and grind the onions in the food processor.

○ Heat the ghee in a heavy-based wok (*kadhai*); add whole spices and stir till they crackle. Add ginger-garlic paste and sauté till light brown.

○ Add minced onions and sauté till golden brown.

○ Make cashew and melon seed paste by soaking them for 30 minutes in milk and grinding in a food processor. Mix this paste with the onion mixture.

○ Add tomato purée and stir in the powdered spices; stir for about 10-15 minutes.

○ Stir in yoghurt, then add 1 lt water and bring to the boil. Lower heat, cover the wok and keep stirring every 5 minutes for the next 30 minutes till the oil leaves the sides of the wok.

BEVERAGES AND SOUPS

Pudina Chhaj

A yoghurt drink flavoured with mint

Yoghurt (*dahi*) ~ 2 cups / 400 gm
Cumin (*jeera*) seeds, roasted ~ ½ tsp
Rock salt (*kala namak*) ~ ½ tsp
Salt to taste
Dried mint (*pudina*) leaves, ground ~ ¼ tsp
Water, cold ~ 3 cups / 600 ml

Method

○ Blend yoghurt with the other ingredients except water till well mixed.
○ Add chilled water and some ice cubes and blend again for a few seconds.
○ Serve chilled, garnished with 2-3 mint leaves.

Thandai

A rich creamy drink flavoured with saffron

Ingredients   serves: 4

Milk ~ 5 cups / 1 lt
Almonds (*badaam*), soaked in water
for 1 hour, peeled
~ ½ cup / 60 gm
Cashew nuts (*kaju*)
~ 2 tbsp / 30 gm
Soaked for 2 hours and drained:
Melon seeds (*magaz*) ~ ½ cup
Black peppercorns
(*sabut kali mirch*) ~ 10-15

Poppy seeds (*khus khus*)
~ 6 tsp / 12 gm
Green cardamom (*choti elaichi*) ~ 10
Aniseed (*saunf*) ~ 2 tsp / 3 gm

Sugar ~ 10 tbsp / 200 gm
Rose water (*gulab jal*)
~ 1 tbsp / 15 ml
Saffron (*kesar*), soaked in
1 tbsp water ~ a few strands

Method

○ Blend almonds, cashew nuts, and the drained ingredients to a smooth paste with a little milk.
○ Mix the paste in the remaining milk. Add sugar and blend again. Strain the mixture through a muslin cloth.
○ Add rose water and mix well.
○ Serve chilled, garnished with saffron strands.

Pudina Ka Thanda

Mint cooler

Ingredients serves: 4

Mint (*pudina*) leaves, minced ~ ¼ cup
Water ~ 4 cups / 800 ml
Juice of lemons (*nimbu*), fresh ~ 4
Sugar ~ 6 tbsp / 120 gm
Black salt (*kala namak*) ~ ½ tsp
Rose water (*gulab jal*) ~ ¼ tsp

Method

○ Blend all the ingredients together for about 2 minutes or till well mixed.
○ Serve chilled, garnished with fresh mint leaves.

Mulligatawny Soup

Tamarind soup

Ingredients   serves: 4

Ghee ~ 1 tsp / 5 gm

Dry red chillies (*sookhi lal mirch*) ~ 2

Coriander (*dhaniya*) seeds ~ 1 tbsp / 6 gm

Cumin (*jeera*) seeds ~ 1 tsp / 2 gm

Black pepper (*kali mirch*) powder ~ ¼ tsp

Garlic (*lasan*) cloves, peeled ~ 2

Madras onions ~ 2

Mint (*pudina*) leaves ~ a few

Curry leaves (*kadhi patta*) ~ a few

Green coriander (*hara dhaniya*), finely chopped ~ 1 tbsp / 4 gm

Tamarind (*imli*), extract, lemon-sized ~ 2½ cups

Salt to taste

Asafoetida (*hing*) ~ a pinch

Soft cooked rice (along with cooked water) ~ 2 tbsp

Method

○ Heat the ghee in a pan; add dry red chillies, coriander seeds, cumin seeds, and black pepper powder; sauté till golden. Remove from heat and keep aside to cool.

○ Grind this mixture coarsely and add garlic, Madras onions, mint, and curry leaves; pound again.

○ Tie the mixture in a clean muslin cloth along with green coriander.

○ Dilute the tamarind extract with enough water. Add salt and spice bag. Cook on low heat till the mixture comes to the boil.

○ Add asafoetida and cooked rice along with water in which the rice has been cooked; mix well. Remove from heat and cover with a lid. After some time squeeze the spice bag and remove.

○ Reheat and serve hot in small cups, along with crisp poppadums.

Papita Shorba

Raw papaya soup

Ingredients serves: 4

Papaya (*papita*), raw, chopped ~ 1 cup

Carrot (*gajar*), finely diced ~ 1

Butter ~ 1 tbsp / 20 gm

Bay leaf (*tej patta*) ~ 1

Onion, chopped ~ 1

For the spice bag:
Crush the ingredients coarsely and tie in a clean muslin cloth

Ginger (*adrak*), ½" piece ~ 1

Cumin (*jeera*) seeds ~ ½ tsp

Salt, sugar, and black pepper (*kali mirch*) to taste

Cheese, grated, to taste

Method

○ Heat the butter in a pressure pan or cooker; add bay leaf and onion. Lower heat and sauté for 1-2 minutes. Add carrot and papaya. Sauté on medium heat for another 2 minutes. Pour just enough water to cover the pieces. Add the spice bag and close the lid. Lower heat and pressure cook till first whistle.

○ Remove the cooker from the heat and keep aside to cool. Discard the spice bag and blend the mixture to a smooth paste.

○ Strain the mixture and dilute with water to get the right consistency.

○ Add salt, sugar, and black pepper to taste.

○ Reheat and serve hot garnished with cheese and accompanied with bread sticks.

Note: Soup tastes better if half-ripe and firm papaya is used.

Zakir Hussain (third president of India) with Kundan Lal Gujral.

Field Marshall Sam Maneckshaw and his wife with Kundan Lal Gujral.

NON VEGETARIAN

Tandoori Murgh

Tandoori chicken

Ingredients   serves: 4

Chicken, cut into 4 pieces,
washed, pat dried ~ 1 (750 gm)
For the first marinade:
Lemon (*nimbu*) juice
~ 1½ tbsp / 22 ml
Red chill powder ~ 1 tsp / 2 gm
Salt to taste
For the second marinade:
Yoghurt (*dahi*) ~ ½ cup / 100 gm
Garlic (*lasan*) paste ~ 1 tbsp / 18 gm
Ginger (*adrak*) paste
~ 1 tbsp / 18 gm

Rock salt (*kala namak*)
~ ½ tsp
Garam masala (see p. 24)
~ 1 tsp / 2 gm
Red colour ~ a few drops
Salt to taste

Dry fenugreek (*kasoori methi*) leaves,
powdered ~ ½ tsp
Onions, cut into rings ~ 2
Lemon (*nimbu*), cut into
wedges ~ 1

Method

○ Make 2 deep incisions each on the breasts, thighs, and drumsticks.
○ For the first marinade, mix all the ingredients and rub over the chicken pieces and also inside the incisions. Keep aside for 1 hour.
○ For the second marinade, mix all the ingredients in a bowl and rub into the chicken pieces; keep aside for 3-4 hours to marinate.
○ Preheat the oven at 180°C / 350°F. Place the chicken on the grill rack or wire rack (place a tray underneath to collect the drippings) and grill for 8-10 minutes. Brush the pieces with oil, turn them around and grill for 8-10 minutes more till the chicken is dry and cooked. Remove from oven, sprinkle dry fenugreek powder and serve with onion rings and lemon wedges.

Murgh Lababdar

Chicken in a creamy tomato gravy

Ingredients serves: 4

Reshmi kebab (see p. 52) ~ 14
Refined oil ~ 3 tbsp / 45 ml
Ginger-garlic (*adrak-lasan*)
paste ~ 1 tbsp / 18 gm
Onions, finely chopped ~ 2
Tomatoes, chopped ~ 2
Capsicum (*Shimla mirch*),
finely chopped ~ 2
Salt to taste
White pepper (*safed mirch*)

powder ~ 1 tsp / 2 gm
Cumin (*jeera*) powder
~ 1 tsp / 1½ gm
Red chilli powder ~ 1 tsp / 2 gm
Vegetable gravy (see p. 26)
~ 1 cup / 200 ml
Tomato purée, fresh
~ 1 cup / 200 ml
Butter ~ 5 tsp / 25 gm
Cream, fresh ~ 1 cup / 200 ml

Method

○ Heat the oil in a pan; add ginger-garlic paste and onions; sauté for 4-5 minutes or till onions turn golden brown.

○ Add tomatoes, capsicum, and the spices; sauté for 8-10 minutes or till the oil leaves the sides of the pan.

○ Add *reshmi* kebab and stir for 5 minutes.

○ Stir in the vegetable gravy and tomato purée; mix well for about 8-10 minutes.

○ Add butter and stir till it melts. Stir in the cream; and serve hot.

Dhaniya Murgh

Easy-to-cook chicken flavoured with coriander

Ingredients serves: 4

Chicken, cut into pieces
~ 1 kg approx.
Tomato purée ~ 1 cup / 200 ml
Coriander (*dhaniya*) powder
~ ½ cup
Salt ~ 1½ tsp / 6 gm
Garam masala (see p. 24)
~ 1 tsp / 2 gm

Red chilli powder ~ 1½ tsp / 3 gm
Garlic (*lasan*) paste
~ 2 tsp / 12 gm
Ginger (*adrak*) paste
~ 2 tsp / 12 gm
Sugar (optional) ~ 1 tsp / 3 gm
Green coriander (*hara dhaniya*),
chopped for garnishing

Method

○ Heat a non-stick pan; add tomato purée, chicken, and the remaining ingredients except green coriander. Mix well. Add ½ cup water. Lower heat and cook covered for 4-5 minutes. Remove cover and stir once. Continue to cook till the chicken is tender.

○ Increase heat and cook till the preparation is dry (you can keep a little gravy or make it dry as per choice).

○ Serve hot garnished with green coriander.

Murgh Pakora

Batter-fried chicken

Ingredients serves: 4

Chicken, cut into 8 pieces
~ 750 gm
Lemon (*nimbu*) juice
~ 1 tbsp / 15 ml
Ginger-garlic (*adrak-lasan*)
paste ~ 1 tsp / 6 gm
Salt to taste
Red chilli powder
~ ½ tsp

For the batter:
Egg ~ 1
Gram flour (*besan*)
~ 5 tbsp / 50 gm
Refined flour (*maida*)
~ 1 tbsp / 15 gm
Salt and black pepper to taste
Refined oil for deep-frying
Chaat masala (see p. 25) ~ ½ tsp

Method

○ Make deep incisions on the chicken pieces.

○ Marinate the chicken with lemon juice, ginger-garlic paste, salt, and red chilli powder for about 30 minutes.

○ For the batter, mix all the ingredients together in a blender.

○ Heat the oil in a wok *(kadhai)*; dip the marinated chicken in the batter and then lower gently in the hot oil. Deep-fry on medium heat till light brown. Remove with a slotted spoon, prick each piece with a fork and keep aside for 10 minutes.

○ Fry the pieces again till golden brown. Remove and drain the excess oil on absorbent paper towels.

○ Sprinkle *chaat* masala before serving.

Murgh Tikka Masala

Spicy chicken cooked in the oven

Ingredients serves: 4

Chicken, boneless ~ 750 gm
For the first marinade:
Lemon juice ~ 1½ tbsp / 22 ml
Salt ~ 1 tsp / 4 gm
For the second marinade:
Yoghurt (*dahi*) ~ ½ cup / 100 gm
Garlic (*lasan*) paste ~ 1 tbsp / 18 gm
Ginger (*adrak*) paste
~ 1 tbsp / 18 gm
Garam masala (see p. 24) ~ ½ tsp
Salt ~ ½ tsp
White pepper (*safed mirch*)
powder ~ ½ tsp
Red chilli powder ~ 1 tsp / 2 gm
Cumin (*jeera*) powder
~ 1 tsp / 1½ gm
Refined oil ~ a few drops
Salt to taste
For the masala:
Refined oil ~ 2 tbsp / 30 ml

Onion, chopped ~ 1
Ginger paste ~ 1 tbsp / 18 gm
Garlic paste ~ 1 tbsp / 18 gm
Cumin powder ~ 1 tsp / 1½ gm
Coriander (*dhaniya*)
powder ~ 1 tsp / 1½ gm
Turmeric (*haldi*) powder
~ 1 tsp / 2 gm
Red chilli powder ~ 2 tsp / 4 gm
Garam masala ~ 1 tsp / 2 gm
Salt to taste
Green chilli, chopped ~ 1
Tomato purée
~ 1½ cups / 300 ml
Lemon (*nimbu*) juice
~ 1 tbsp / 15 ml
Butter ~ 2½ tbsp / 50 gm
Cream ~ ½ cup / 100 ml
Green coriander (*hara dhaniya*),
chopped ~ 1 tbsp / 4 gm

Method

○ For the first marinade, mix all the ingredients together and rub into the chicken; keep aside for half an hour.
○ For the second marinade, mix all the ingredients in a bowl. Add the marinated chicken, mix well and keep aside for another 3-4 hours.

- Put the marinated chicken in a preheated oven set at 180°C / 350°F for about 10 minutes. Brush the chicken with oil and put it back in the oven for another 10 minutes. Remove and keep aside.
- For the masala, heat the oil in a pan; add onion and sauté till golden brown. Mix in ginger-garlic paste and sauté for about 2-3 minutes.
- Stir in all the spices and salt. Add the cooked chicken and sauté for 4-5 minutes.
- Add green chilli, tomato purée and lemon juice; stir for another 4-5 minutes. Add butter and stir for 2-3 minutes. Mix in the cream.
- Serve hot garnished with green coriander.

Father of Tandoori Cuisine

British foreign secretary, Sir Robin Cook, while addressing a think tank in London in April 2001, claimed that the murgh tikka *masala was one of Britain's true national dishes. This led to great speculation regarding the origin of this awesome and delicious dish. The majority of votes indicated that it is a derivative of butter chicken, introduced by Kundan Lal Gujral, almost 60 years ago.*

Saag Murgh

Chicken cooked with spinach

Ingredients serves: 4

Chicken, cut into 8 pieces
~ 750 gm
Spinach (*palak*), stems trimmed,
finely chopped, washed in plenty of
water ~ 1 kg
Refined oil ~ 5-6 tbsp / 75-90 ml
Onions, finely chopped ~ 3
Ginger-garlic (*adrak-lasan*)
paste ~ 3 tbsp / 54 gm
Green cardamom (*choti elaichi*) ~ 2
Bay leaves (*tej patta*) ~ 2

Tomato purée ~ ¾ cup / 150 ml
Yoghurt (*dahi*), thick,
beaten well ~ ½ cup / 100 gm
Salt to taste
Red chilli powder ~ 1 tsp / 2 gm
Garam masala (see p. 24)
~ 1 tsp / 2 gm
Milk ~ ½ cup / 100 ml
Cream, fresh ~ 3 tbsp / 60 ml
Ginger (*adrak*), ½" piece,
julienned ~ 1

Method

○ Blend the spinach with a little water.

○ Heat the oil in a heavy-bottomed pan; add onions and sauté till golden brown. Add ginger-garlic paste and cook for a minute. Add green cardamom, bay leaves, and tomato purée; cook for 2-3 minutes. Add yoghurt, salt, red chilli powder, and garam masala; cook, stirring continuously, on high heat till the oil separates.

○ Add chicken and stir-fry on high heat till the chicken turns light brown and the spices coat the pieces.

○ Add spinach, stirring the entire mixture on high heat till all the water evaporates. Stir in the milk. Reduce heat, and cook covered till the chicken is tender. Remove the lid from the vessel and cook for another 2-3 minutes. Add cream and stir.

○ Serve garnished with ginger.

Murgh Navrattan Korma

Spicy chicken garnished with dried fruits

Ingredients serves: 4

Chicken, cut into 8 pieces ~ 750 gm

Refined oil ~ 3 tbsp / 45 ml

Unsalted butter ~ 2½ tbsp / 50 gm

Bay leaf (*tej patta*) ~ 1

Cinnamon (*dalchini*), 1" sticks ~ 5

Cloves (*laung*) ~ 6

Green cardamom (*choti elaichi*) ~ 10

Onions, grated ~ 1 cup / 120 gm

Garlic (*lasan*) paste ~ 2 tbsp / 36 gm

Ginger (*adrak*) paste ~ 2 tbsp / 36 gm

Turmeric (*haldi*) powder

~ 1 tsp / 2 gm

Red chilli powder ~ 2 tsp / 4 gm

Almond (*badaam*) paste

~ 1 tbsp / 15 gm

Salt to taste

Yoghurt (*dahi*), whisked

~ 4 tbsp / 120 gm

Cream ~ 1 cup / 200 ml

Green chillies, slit into half ~ 3

Mace (*javitri*) powder

~ 1 tsp / 2 gm

Vetivier (*kewda*) essence ~ 3 drops

For the garnishing:

Almonds, peeled ~ 2 tbsp / 30 gm

Cashew nuts (*kaju*) ~ 2 tbsp / 30 gm

Hazel nuts ~ 2 tsp / 10 gm

Pistachios (*pista*) ~ 1 tbsp / 15 gm

Raisins (*kishmish*) ~ 1 tbsp / 10 gm

Black cumin (*shah jeera*) seeds,

roasted, powdered ~ 2-3 tsp

Saffron (*kesar*), soaked in

2 tsp warm milk ~ a few strands

Ginger, fresh, julienned

~ 1 tsp / 6 gm

Mint (*pudina*) leaves, fresh ~ 2-3

Method

○ Heat the oil and butter in a pan; add bay leaf, cinnamon sticks, cloves, and green cardamom; sauté over medium heat until they begin to crackle.

○ Add onions and sauté for a few minutes. Add ginger-garlic paste, turmeric powder, red chilli powder, almond paste, salt, and yoghurt. Cook over medium heat for 5-10 minutes until the oil separates from the mixture.

○ Add chicken, stir and cook over medium heat for about 25 minutes, till the chicken is tender.

○ Stir in cream, green chillies, mace powder, and vetivier essence.

○ Fry all the dried fruits in butter; add black cumin powder and saffron; mix well. Garnish the dish with the dried fruit mixture. Top with ginger and mint leaves.

Birth of Tandoori Chicken

During my late teens, when I started working part time with my grandfather, Kundan Lal, in the restaurant, I asked him how he invented the tandoori chicken. He said that one evening after a hard day's work, his master, Mukha Singh, requested a light and dry chicken dish for dinner. Determined to please his mentor, he took a chicken marinated it with yoghurt, salt, pepper, and red chilli powder and put it in the tandoor (those days used only for cooking tandoori rotis). He took an iron wire used to hang clothes for drying as a skewer and pierced it through the chicken. He also skewered a raw onion at the end of the wire. Slowly, he lowered the wire holding the chicken in the tandoor and what came out was tandoori chicken. This is how tandoori cuisine was created.

Murgh-e-Shaan

Stuffed chicken drumsticks

Ingredients serves: 4

Chicken legs, whole ~ 4
For the marinade:
Ginger (*adrak*) paste
~ 2 tbsp / 36 gm
Garlic (*lasan*) paste ~ 2 tbsp / 36 gm
Green chilli paste ~ 2 tbsp / 30 gm
Salt to taste
Lemon (*nimbu*) juice ~ 2 tbsp / 30 ml
For the stuffing:
Almonds (*badaam*),
chopped ~ 3 tbsp / 45 gm

Chicken mince ~ 300 gm
Cashew nuts (*kaju*),
chopped ~ 3 tbsp / 45 gm
Mint (*pudina*) chutney
(see p. 107) ~ ½ cup
Garam masala (see p. 24)
~ 1 tsp / 2 gm

Refined oil ~ 3 tbsp / 45 ml
Saffron (*kesar*) ~ 1 tsp / 1 gm
Cream ~ ½ cup / 100 ml

Method

- Debone the entire chicken leg, leaving only the top of the drumstick. Flatten the chicken leg using a steak hammer.
- For the marinade, mix half the quantity each of ginger, garlic, green chilli pastes, salt, and lemon juice; rub the paste into the chicken legs and refrigerate for half an hour.
- For the stuffing, mix all the ingredients and the remaining ginger, garlic, green chilli pastes, salt, and lemon juice.
- Stuff the deboned chicken with this mixture, rolling the chicken in such a way that the mince is wrapped in it.
- Place the stuffed chicken on a greased tray and cover with aluminium foil. Bake in a medium-hot oven for about 15 minutes or till cooked. Remove and slice each diagonally. Pour saffron mixed with cream over the chicken. Serve with cut lemon and tomato.

Khatta Murgh

Tangy chicken

Ingredients serves: 4

Chicken, deboned ~ 1 kg

For the marinade:

Yoghurt (*dahi*) ~ 1¼ cups / 250 gm

Ginger (*adrak*) paste
~ 2 tbsp / 36 gm

Garlic (*lasan*) paste
~ 2 tbsp / 36 gm

Cumin (*jeera*) seeds ~ 1 tsp / 2 gm

Black pepper (*kali mirch*)
powder ~ 1 tsp / 2 gm

Lemon (*nimbu*) juice
~ 2 tbsp / 30 ml

Green chillies, chopped ~ 3

Almond (*badaam*) paste
~ 3 tbsp / 45 gm

Onions, cut into rings
~ ¾ cup / 150 gm

Capsicum (*Shimla mirch*),
cut into rings ~ 100 gm

White butter ~ 2½ tbsp / 50 gm

Saffron (*kesar*), dissolved in
1 tbsp milk ~ a pinch

Salt to taste

Method

○ For the marinade, mix all the ingredients and rub into the chicken. Keep aside for 2 hours.

○ Place the chicken without overlapping in a greased, ovenproof shallow dish. Arrange onion and capsicum rings over the chicken and pour the leftover marinade, evenly.

○ Dot with white butter and roast in a preheated oven (150°C / 300°F) for about 20 minutes.

○ Remove the dish from the oven, sprinkle saffron, cover the dish and return back to the oven. Simmer for about 10 minutes more.

○ Uncover the dish, wipe the edges and simmer again for about 10 minutes. Serve hot with mint chutney (see p. 107).

Balti Murgh

Chicken flavoured with onion seeds

Ingredients serves: 4

Chicken breasts, cut into small pieces
~ 500 gm

Corn oil ~ 4-5 tbsp / 60-75 ml

Onions, sliced ~ 2

Onion seeds (*kalonji*) ~ ½ tsp

Curry leaves (*kadhi patta*) ~ 5

Coriander (*dhaniya*)
powder ~ 1 tsp / 1½ gm

Garlic (*lasan*) paste ~ 1 tsp / 6 gm

Red chilli powder ~ ½ tsp

Turmeric (*haldi*) powder
~ ½ tsp

Salt ~ 1 tsp / 4 gm

Fenugreek (*methi*) leaves,
chopped ~ 1½ tbsp / 3 gm

Red peppers, large, cored, deseeded,
cut into slices ~ 2

Lemon (*nimbu*) juice
~ 1 tbsp / 15 ml

Cream, fresh ~ 1 tbsp / 20 ml

Method

○ Heat the oil in a heavy-bottomed pan; add onions, onion seeds, and curry leaves; sauté for 2-3 minutes. Lower heat and add coriander powder, garlic paste, red chilli powder, turmeric powder, salt, and the chicken. Stir-fry for 10-12 minutes.

○ Add fenugreek leaves and red pepper; mix well. Cook for 5-6 minutes then add lemon juice; cook till the chicken is tender.

○ Serve hot garnished with cream.

Murgh Malai

Creamy chicken

Ingredients   serves: 4

Chicken, cut into 8 pieces, make incisions on the pieces ~ 750 gm
For the marinade:
Yoghurt (*dahi*) ~ ¾ cup / 150 gm
Ginger (*adrak*) paste ~ 2 tbsp / 36 gm
Garlic (*lasan*) paste ~ 1 tbsp / 18 gm
Red chilli powder ~ ½ tsp
Salt to taste

Refined oil ~ 5-6 tbsp / 75-90 ml
Bay leaf (*tej patta*) ~ 1
Green cardamom (*choti elaichi*) ~ 3-4
Black cumin (*shah jeera*) seeds ~ ½ tsp

Onions, large, ground to a paste ~ 3
Cashew nuts (*kaju*), soaked in ¼ cup warm milk for 15-20 minutes, ground to a smooth paste ~ ½ cup / 60 gm
Milk ~ 1 cup / 200 ml
Cream, fresh ~ ½ cup / 100 ml
Garam masala (see p. 24) ~ 1 tsp / 2 gm
Saffron (*kesar*) ~ a few strands
Green coriander (*hara dhaniya*), chopped for garnishing

Method

○ For the marinade, mix all the ingredients and rub into the chicken. Keep aside for about 2 hours.

○ Heat the oil in a pan; add bay leaf, green cardamom, and black cumin seeds. Sauté for about a minute. Add onion paste and stir till light brown. Stir in the chicken with the marinade and cook on high heat for about 5 minutes.

○ Add cashew nut paste, stirring continuously, on medium heat, till juices from the chicken evaporate and the oil separates. Add milk and ½ cup water, cover the pan and cook till the chicken is tender.

○ Stir in the cream. Serve hot garnished with garam masala, saffron, and green coriander.

Murgh Ajwaindar

Chicken flavoured with carom seeds

Chicken, cut into 8 pieces, make
incisions on the pieces ~ 750 gm
For the marinade:
Yoghurt (*dahi*) ~ ½ cup / 100 gm
Carom seeds (*ajwain*) ~ 2 tsp / 4 gm
Salt to taste
Red chilli powder ~ 1 tsp / 2 gm
Black salt (*kala namak*) ~ ½ tsp

Garam masala (see p. 24) ~ 1 tsp / 2 gm
Ginger (*adrak*) paste ~ 1 tbsp / 18 gm
Garlic (*lasan*) paste ~ 1 tbsp / 18 gm

Refined oil ~ 3 tbsp / 45 ml
Cream ~ 3 tbsp / 60 ml
Green coriander (*hara dhaniya*),
chopped for garnishing

Method

○ For the marinade, mix all the ingredients together and rub into the chicken pieces. Keep in the fridge for about 1 hour.

○ Heat the oil in a heavy-bottomed pan; add chicken along with the leftover marinade. Cook on high heat till the juices evaporate and the chicken browns evenly.

○ Add ½ cup water, cover the pan with a lid and cook on low heat, till the chicken becomes tender.

○ Add cream and green coriander and stir till the chicken is coated with the mixture.

○ Serve hot with mint chutney (see p. 107).

Murgh Nargisi

Chicken kebabs

Ingredients   serves: 4

Chicken, boneless ~ 750 gm
Grind to a smooth paste:
Onion, sliced ~ 1
Green coriander (*hara dhaniya*),
chopped ~ 2 tbsp / 8 gm
Green chillies, fresh ~ 2
Ginger-garlic (*adrak-lasan*)
paste ~ 2 tbsp / 36 gm
Salt ~ 2 tsp / 8 gm

Black pepper (*kali mirch*)
powder ~ ½ tsp
Coriander (*dhaniya*) powder
~ 1 tsp / 1½ gm
Cheese spread ~ 2 tbsp / 30 gm

Eggs, beaten ~ 2
Breadcrumbs ~ 3 tbsp / 45 gm
Refined oil ~ 1 cup / 200 ml

Method

○ Boil the chicken till tender and then mince it in the grinder and keep aside.

○ Mix the minced chicken with the spice paste. Divide the mixture equally into lemon-sized balls. Flatten them to 2"-long kebab. Keep aside.

○ Dip the kebab in the egg and then coat with breadcrumbs. Keep aside.

○ Heat the oil in a pan; fry the kebabs, a few at a time, for about one minute turning them gently with a slotted spoon till golden grown. Remove and drain the excess oil on absorbent paper towels.

○ Serve hot with mint chutney (see p. 107).

Y B Chavan (former cabinet minister) and Mr Dhupia (standing first from right) founder member of Chelmsford Club with Kundan Lal Gujral.

Swaran Singh (former chief minister) with Kundan Lal Gujral.

Murgh Musallam

Chicken in a creamy tomato gravy

Ingredients serves: 4

Chicken, cut into 8 pieces ~ 700 gm
Minced lamb, parboiled ~ 200 gm
Lamb kidney, parboiled
~ 100 gm
For the marinade: mix together
Yoghurt (*dahi*), drained
~ 2½ cups / 500 gm
Salt to taste
Red chilli powder ~ 2½ tsp / 5 gm
Coriander (*dhaniya*) powder
~ 3 tsp / 5 gm
Vinegar (*sirka*) ~ 1½ tsp / 8 ml

Refined oil ~ 1 cup / 200 ml
Bay leaves (*tej patta*) ~ 2
Ginger-garlic (*adrak-lasan*) paste
~ 5 tsp / 30 gm

Black cumin (*shah jeera*)
seeds ~ 1 tsp / 2 gm
Brown onion paste, sliced, deep-fried
till golden brown, blended with little
water ~ 500 gm
Tomato purée, peeled, blanched,
blended ~ 500 gm
Cumin (*jeera*) powder ~ 3 tsp / 5 gm
Red chilli powder ~ 2½ tsp / 5 gm
Garam masala (see p. 24) ~ 15 gm
Yoghurt (*dahi*) ~ ¼ cup / 50 gm
Water ~ 1 cup / 200 ml
Butter ~ 5 tbsp / 100 gm
Cream, fresh ~ 1 cup / 200 ml
Egg, hard-boiled, halved ~ 1
Tomato, cut into 4 pieces ~ 1
Green chillies, slit ~ 2

Method

○ Marinate the chicken with the marinade for an hour.

○ Heat the oil; sauté bay leaves and ginger-garlic paste for a minute.
Add black cumin seeds and sauté again. Stir in brown onion paste;
sauté for 1-2 minutes. Add chicken, stir for 7-8 minutes. Add lamb
and kidney and mix for 5 minutes. Stir in the tomato purée.

○ Add spices, yoghurt, and water. Cook covered till the chicken is
tender. Stir in the butter. When it melts add cream gradually. Serve
garnished with egg, tomato, and green chillies.

Kasturi Kebab

Chicken kebab flavoured with dried fenugreek

Ingredients serves: 4

Chicken, boneless ~ 600 gm

Ginger-garlic (*adrak-lasan*) paste
~ 2 tsp / 12 gm

Vinegar (*sirka*) ~ 1 tbsp / 15 ml

Salt ~ ½ tsp

Refined oil ~ 2 tbsp / 30 ml

Garlic (*lasan*), chopped
~ 1 tsp / 3 gm

Gram flour (*besan*)
~ 2½ tbsp / 25 gm

Eggs ~ 2

Cardamom (*elaichi*) powder
~ 2 tsp / 4 gm

Salt to taste

White pepper (*safed mirch*) powder
~ 2 tsp / 4 gm

Breadcrumbs ~ 1 tbsp / 15 gm

Dried fenugreek leaves (*kasoori methi*) ~ 1 tbsp / 4 gm

Cream ~ 1 tbsp / 20 ml

Method

○ Rub the chicken with ginger-garlic paste, vinegar, and salt. Keep aside for about an hour.

○ Heat the oil in a wok (*kadhai*); add garlic and sauté till light brown. Add gram flour and stir continuously for about 8-10 minutes till the oil separates. Remove and keep aside to cool for about an hour.

○ In a bowl, add the gram flour mixture, 1 egg, cardamom powder, salt, and white pepper; mix the marinade well.

○ Marinate the chicken with this marinade and keep aside for half an hour. Put on skewers and roast in a moderately hot tandoor for about 6-7 minutes. Alternatively bake in a preheated oven at 180°C / 350°F. Baste with a little oil after 5 minutes and turn the side.

○ After 10 minutes or when nearly cooked, coat the chicken with a mixture of 1 egg, breadcrumbs, and dry fenugreek leaves and cook for about 3-4 minutes. Serve hot with mint chutney (see p. 107).

Afghani Murgh

Succulent cheesy chicken kebab

Ingredients   serves: 4

Chicken, cut into 8 pieces ~ 600 gm
Ginger-garlic (*adrak-lasan*) paste
~ 2 tsp / 12 gm
Vinegar (*sirka*) ~ 1 tbsp / 15 ml
Salt ~ ½ tsp
Cashew nuts (*kaju*)
~ 3½ tbsp / 50 gm
Milk ~ ¼ cup / 50 ml

Cheese, grated ~ 2 tbsp / 30 gm
Cardamom (*elaichi*) powder
~ 2 tsp / 4 gm
Salt to taste
White pepper (*safed mirch*) powder
~ 2 tsp / 4 gm
Eggs ~ 2
Cream ~ 2½ tbsp / 50 ml

Method

○ Make incisions on the chicken and rub it thoroughly with ginger-garlic paste, vinegar, and salt. Keep aside for half an hour.

○ Blend the cashew nut with milk and make a smooth paste.

○ Mix cheese, cardamom powder, salt, and white pepper with the cashew paste. Add eggs and mix well into a smooth paste.

○ Marinate the chicken with this mixture and keep aside for about an hour.

○ Put on skewers and roast it in a moderately hot tandoor for 6-7 minutes. Then baste with oil, turn upside down and further grill till chicken is tender. Alternatively cook in a preheated oven at 180°C / 350°F.

○ Serve hot with mint chutney (see p. 107).

Reshmi Kebab

Succulent chicken kebabs marinated in cream and cheese

Ingredients serves: 4

Chicken, deboned, cut into 14
pieces ~ 750 gm
Ginger-garlic (*adrak-lasan*)
paste ~ 1½ tsp / 10 gm
Salt ~ 1½ tsp / 6 gm
Salad oil ~ 2 tbsp / 30 ml
Gram flour (*besan*) ~ 5 tbsp / 50 gm

Cream ~ ½ cup / 100 gm
White pepper (*safed mirch*) powder
~ 2 tsp / 4 gm
Cheese spread ~ ¼ cup / 50 gm
Egg ~ 1
Green cardamom (*elaichi*) powder
~ 1 tsp / 2 gm

Method

o   Marinate the chicken with ginger-garlic paste and salt. Keep aside
for 1 hour.

o   Heat the oil in a heavy-bottomed pan; add gram flour and
stir continuously till the oil separates and a sweet smell
emanates. Remove from heat, add cream, white pepper powder,
cheese spread, egg, and green cardamom powder. Whisk to a
smooth paste.

o   Apply to the chicken and keep aside for 2 hours.

o   Skewer the chicken and preferably grill in a tandoor or a preheated
oven till golden brown.

o   Serve with mint chutney (see p. 107) and onion *lachha* in vinegar.

Murgh Chaat

Chicken salad

Ingredients serves: 4

Chicken breasts, large, boiled,
cubed, washed ~ 2
Tomato, small, pulp removed,
cubed ~ 1
Capsicum (*Shimla mirch*), deseeded,
cut into small cubes ~ ½
Spring onions without the greens,
tender, cut into rings ~ 2

Chaat masala (see p. 25)
~ 1 tsp / 2 gm
Rock salt (*kala namak*)
~ ½ tsp
Powdered sugar ~ ¼ tsp
Salt and black pepper (*kali mirch*)
to taste
Juice of lemon (*nimbu*) ~ 1

Method

○ Boil the chicken with ½ tsp salt and ½ cup water till tender or pressure cook to give a whistle.
○ Mix the chicken and the vegetables in a bowl. Sprinkle all the dry ingredients.
○ Add lemon juice and toss well.
○ Cover and refrigerate till chilled.
○ Serve on a bed of lettuce or cabbage.

Note: If the *chaat* is not covered, the chicken will harden.

Tandoori Batyer

Roasted quail

Ingredients serves: 4

Quails (*batyer*) ~ 6 / 150 gm each
Salt to taste
Vinegar (*sirka*) ~ 4 tbsp / 60 ml
Ginger-garlic (*adrak-lasan*) paste
~ 4 tsp / 24 gm
Yoghurt (*dahi*) ~ 2 tbsp / 60 gm
Red chilli powder ~ 2 tsp / 4 gm
Red chilli paste ~ 2 tbsp / 30 gm

Rock salt ~ ½ tsp
Garam masala (see p. 24)
~ 4 tsp / 8 gm
Cumin (*jeera*) powder
~ 1 tbsp
Nutmeg (*jaiphal*) powder
~ 1 tsp / 2 gm
Butter ~ 3 tbsp / 60 gm

Method

○ Clean the quails and rub them with salt, vinegar, and ginger-garlic paste. Keep aside for half an hour.

○ Whisk yoghurt; add red chili powder, red chili paste, and all the spices. Coat the quails with this marinade evenly and keep aside for an hour.

○ Skewer the quails and roast in a moderately hot tandoor for 6-7 minutes. Remove and baste with butter and roast again for 4-5 minutes. Alternatively cook in a preheated oven at 180°C / 350°F.

○ Remove from skewers and serve hot with mint chutney (see p. 107).

Chaamp

Lamb chops

Ingredients   serves: 4

Lamb chops (*chaamp*), beaten,
flattened ~ 12
For the marinade:
Ginger (*adrak*) paste ~ ½ tsp / 3 gm
Garlic (*lasan*) paste ~ 1 tsp / 6 gm
Lemon (*nimbu*) juice
~ 2 tbsp / 30 ml
Black pepper (*kali mirch*)
powder ~ 1 tbsp

Salt ~ 1 tsp / 4 gm
Refined oil ~ 1 cup / 200 ml
Eggs, beaten ~ 2
Breadcrumbs ~ 2 cups / 240 gm
Lemon (*nimbu*), cut into
wedges ~ 4
Tomatoes, cut into wedges ~ 4
Green coriander (*hara dhaniya*),
chopped ~ 1 tbsp / 4 gm

Method

○ For the marinade, mix all the ingredients upto salt and rub into the lamb chops. Keep aside for 30 minutes.

○ Heat the oil in a heavy-bottomed pan; dip the chops in the egg, coat with breadcrumbs and then shallow-fry, 3-4 chops at a time, for 2-3 minutes on each side, until fully cooked. Remove and repeat till all the chops are fried.

○ Serve garnished with lemon and tomato wedges and sprinkled with green coriander.

Khatta Gosht

Tamarind in spicy lamb preparation

Ingredients serves: 4

Lamb, boneless ~ 500 gm
Corn oil ~ 6-7 tbsp / 90-105 ml
Green chillies, deseeded ~ 3-4
Onions, chopped ~ 2
Curry leaves (*kadhi patta*) ~ 5-6
Onion seeds (*kalonji*) ~ ¼ tsp
Ginger (*adrak*) paste ~ 1 tsp / 6 gm
Garlic (*lasan*) paste ~ 1 tsp / 6 gm
Mix with 1 cup water:
Red chilli powder
~ 1 tsp / 2 gm

Salt ~ 1 tsp / 4 gm
Coriander (*dhaniya*) powder
~ 1½ tsp / 2 gm
Cumin (*jeera*) seeds ~ 1 tsp / 2 gm
Tomato purée ~ 1 tbsp / 15 ml
Sugar ~ 1 tbsp / 20 gm

Water ~ 3¼ cups / 650 ml
Tamarind (*imli*) paste ~ ½ tsp
Green coriander (*hara dhaniya*),
chopped ~ 2 tbsp / 8 gm

Method

○ Heat the oil in a heavy-bottomed pan; add green chillies and sauté. Remove with a slotted spoon and keep aside. Add onions, curry leaves, and onion seeds; sauté on medium heat for a few minutes and then add ginger-garlic paste, stirring continuously.

○ Add lamb and stir for a few minutes on low heat.

○ Pour the spice mixture in the pan, increase heat and cook till the mixture comes to the boil. Pour the water and mix well. Lower heat and cook covered for 30 minutes. In between add tamarind paste and stir.

○ When all the water is evaporated, stir-fry till the oil appears on the sides of the pan and the lamb is cooked through.

○ Serve hot garnished with green coriander.

Gosht Passanda

Spicy lamb in yoghurt based sauce

Ingredients serves: 4

Lamb, cut into 2" x 4"
pieces ~ 750 gm
Refined oil ~ ½ cup / 100 ml
Onions, chopped ~ 1 cup / 120 gm
Ginger (*adrak*), finely chopped
~ 1 tbsp / 25 gm
Garlic (*lasan*) cloves
~ 2 tbsp / 30 gm
Poppy seeds (*khus khus*) ~ 1 tbsp
Black cardamom (*badi elaichi*) ~ 3
Cinnamon (*dalchini*), 1" stick ~ 1
Bay leaf (*tej patta*) ~ 1

Green cardamom (*choti elaichi*) ~ 3
Cloves (*laung*) ~ 7
Yoghurt (*dahi*) ~ 1 cup / 200 gm
Salt to taste
Red chilli powder ~ 2 tsp / 4 gm
Garam masala (see p. 24)
~ 1 tsp / 2 gm
Black pepper (*kali mirch*) powder
~ 1 tsp / 2 gm
Green coriander (*hara dhaniya*),
chopped ~ 2½ tbsp / 10 gm
Cream, fresh ~ ½ cup / 100 ml

Method

- Heat the oil in a heavy-bottomed wok *(kadhai)*; sauté half the onions till golden brown. Remove with a slotted spoon; keep aside.
- Blend the fried onion, the remaining raw onion, ginger, garlic, and poppy seeds with 2 tbsp water.
- Reheat the oil and add the whole spices. Sauté till they crackle. Add onion paste and sauté for about 5 minutes. Add lamb and sauté for 5-7 minutes or till the fat surfaces.
- Add yoghurt and stir for another 5 minutes. Add salt, red chilli powder, garam masala, and black pepper powder; mix well.
- Cover with a lid and cook on medium heat for 15-20 minutes or till the lamb is tender.
- Serve garnished with green coriander and cream.

Gosht Shahi Korma

Lamb cooked in a rich yoghurt sauce

Ingredients serves: 4

Lamb, boneless, cleaned ~ 750 gm
For the marinade:
Coriander (*dhaniya*) seeds
~ 3 tbsp / 18 gm
Onions, chopped ~ ½ cup / 60 gm
Almonds (*badaam*) ~ 2 tbsp / 30 gm
Garlic (*lasan*) paste ~ 2 tbsp / 36 gm

Refined oil ~ 1 cup / 200 ml
Onions, chopped
~ 1¼ cups / 150 gm
Salt ~ 3 tsp / 12 gm
Bay leaf (*tej patta*) ~ 1

Green cardamom (*choti elaichi*) ~ 3
Red chilli powder ~ 1 tsp / 2 gm
Garam masala (see p. 24)
~ 1 tsp / 2 gm
Cashew nuts (*kaju*), soaked in ¼ cup
water, ground to a paste
~ ¹/₃ cup / 40 gm
Yoghurt (*dahi*), beaten
~ 1¼ cups / 250 gm
Cream, fresh ~ 1¼ cups / 250 ml
Saffron (*kesar*), mixed with 1 tbsp
warm milk ~ a pinch
Vetivier (*kewda*) essence ~ 5 drops

Method

○ For the marinade, grind all the ingredients into a smooth paste and rub into the lamb. Keep aside for 2 hours in a cool place.

○ Heat the oil in a heavy-bottomed pan; add onions and sauté till opaque. Add the marinated lamb and sauté till the liquid evaporates.

○ Add salt, bay leaf, green cardamom, red chilli powder, garam masala, and cashew nut paste; mix well, stirring continuously. Add 1 cup water; simmer on low heat till the lamb is three quarter cooked.

○ Add yoghurt and stir continuously till the liquid evaporates. Cover the pan with a lid for 25 minutes and cook on low heat till the lamb is fully cooked and tender. Add cream, saffron mixture, and vetivier essence; mix well. Serve hot garnished with green coriander.

Boti Kebabs

Grilled lamb cubes

Ingredients   serves: 4

Lamb, lean with bones, cubed ~ 1 kg
Papaya pulp (*kachri*) ~ 2 tbsp
For the marinade:
Yoghurt (*dahi*) ~ 4 tbsp / 120 gm
Ginger (*adrak*) paste ~ 2 tbsp / 36 gm
Garlic (*lasan*) paste ~ 2 tbsp / 36 gm
Red chilli powder ~ 2 tsp / 4 gm
Cumin (*jeera*) powder ~ 1 tsp / 1½ gm
Coriander (*dhaniya*) powder
~ 2 tsp / 3 gm
Salt ~ 1½ tsp / 6 gm
Corn oil ~ 5 tbsp / 75 ml

Baby tomatoes ~ 10-12
Baby onions ~ 5-6
Lettuce leaves, chilled ~ 10
Onion, cut into slices ~ 1
Red chillies, fresh, sliced ~ 2
Green chillies ~ 2
Chaat masala (see p. 25) ~ 1 tsp / 2 gm
Mint (*pudina*) leaves, finely chopped
~ 1 tbsp / 4 gm
Green coriander (*hara dhaniya*),
finely chopped ~ 1 tbsp / 4 gm
Lemon (*nimbu*), cut into wedges ~ 2

Method

○ For the marinade, mix all the ingredients (upto salt) together and rub into the lamb cubes. Add papaya pulp and keep aside for at least 4-5 hours.

○ Put the marinated lamb in a preheated oven set at 190°C / 375°F, on the grill rack, for 35-40 minutes. Brush the lamb with oil after 15 minutes, turn the pieces upside down and continue to grill for another 20 minutes or till the lamb is tender.

○ Heat the oil in a pan; sauté baby tomatoes and onions till the outside becomes a little dark. Remove them onto a serving dish. Arrange the lettuce leaves, red and green chillies, and onions along the side of the dish. Add grilled lamb in the centre. Sprinkle *chaat* masala and garnish with mint leaves, green coriander, and lemon.

Nihari Gosht

A Mughlai style lamb preparation

Ingredients serves: 4

Lamb, with bone, cut into 12-13
pieces ~ 1 kg

Refined oil ~ ½ cup / 100 ml

Onions, chopped ~ 2 cups / 240 gm

Green cardamom (*choti elaichi*) ~ 8

Cloves (*laung*) ~ 6-7

Black peppercorns (*sabut kali
mirch*) ~ 12-15

Cinnamon (*dalchini*), ½" sticks ~ 4

Bay leaves (*tej patta*) ~ 2

Coriander (*dhaniya*) powder
~ 4 tsp / 6 gm

Dry red chillies (*sookhi lal
mirch*) ~ 8-10

Turmeric (*haldi*) powder
~ 2 tsp / 4 gm

Ginger (*adrak*) paste ~ 1 tsp / 6 gm

Garlic (*lasan*) paste ~ 1 tsp / 6 gm

Salt to taste

Yoghurt (*dahi*), whisked
~ 1 cup / 200 gm

Mustard (*sarson*) oil ~ 4 tbsp / 60 ml

Refined flour (*maida*)
~ 1 tbsp / 10 gm

Gram flour (*besan*) ~ 1 tbsp / 10 gm

Garam masala (see p. 24)
~ 2 tsp / 4 gm

Fennel (*moti saunf*) seeds
~ 1 tsp / 1½ gm

Lemon (*nimbu*) juice ~ 2 tsp / 10 ml

Vetivier (*kewda*) essence
~ 1 tbsp / 15 ml

Saffron (*kesar*) ~ 1 tsp / 1 gm

Mace (*javitri*) powder ~ 1 tsp / 2 gm

Green coriander (*hara dhaniya*),
chopped ~ 3 tsp

Method

○ Heat the oil in a heavy-bottomed pan; add onions and sauté over
   medium heat till golden brown. Add lamb, green cardamom,
   cloves, black peppercorns, cinnamon sticks, and bay leaves. Cook
   until the water evaporates.

- Add coriander powder, dry red chillies, turmeric powder, ginger paste, garlic paste, and salt. Cook until the oil separates from the mixture.
- Add yoghurt, stirring over high heat for about 10 minutes and then reduce heat to medium. Add 1 lt water and bring to the boil. Lower heat and cook covered, stirring occasionally, until the lamb is tender.
- Now remove the lamb from the gravy and keep aside.
- Heat the mustard oil in a pan; add both the flours and cook on low heat, stirring continuously, until light brown. Now add the lamb gravy and mix well. Remove the pan from the heat. Pass the thickened gravy through a soup strainer and then bring it to the boil again.
- Add lamb, garam masala, fennel powder, lemon juice, vetivier essence, saffron, and mace powder; stir well.
- Serve garnished with green coriander.

A True Punjabi

A person who determinedly took cooking as a hobby, as well as a means to make a living, Kundan Lal Gujral created the famous makhani *gravy. In it went the tandoori chicken, and out came the famous butter chicken—a true Punjabi dish!*

Gosht Dopiazza

Lamb cooked with onions

Ingredients serves: 4

Lamb, cubed ~ 1 kg
Refined oil ~ 1 cup / 200 ml
Bay leaves (*tej patta*) ~ 2
Cinnamon (*dalchini*), ½" sticks ~ 3
Cloves (*laung*) ~ 8
Dry red chillies (*sookhi lal mirch*) ~ 8
Green cardamom (*choti elaichi*) ~ 10
Turmeric (*haldi*) powder
~ 1½ tsp / 3 gm
Onions, sliced ~ 2 cups / 250 gm
Garlic (*lasan*) paste ~ 3 tbsp / 54 gm
Tomatoes, skinned, deseeded,
chopped ~ 400 gm
Madras onions ~ 250 gm
Butter ~ 2½ tbsp / 50 gm

Garam masala (see p. 24) ~ 2 tsp / 4 gm
Coriander (*dhaniya*) powder
~ 2 tsp / 3 gm
Cumin (*jeera*) powder ~ 2 tsp / 3 gm
Mace (*javitri*) powder ~ ½ tsp
Nutmeg (*jaiphal*) powder
~ 2 tsp / 4 gm
Black pepper (*kali mirch*), coarsely
crushed ~ 2 tsp / 4 gm
Salt to taste
Cream, fresh ~ 2½ tbsp / 50 ml
Green coriander (*hara dhaniya*),
chopped ~ 1 tsp
Ginger (*adrak*), julienned
~ 2 tsp / 36 gm

Method

○ Heat the oil in a heavy-bottomed pan; crackle the whole spices and add turmeric powder. Add onions and sauté till golden brown. Then add garlic paste and tomatoes; cook for 5 minutes on high heat.

○ Add lamb, stirring over medium heat for 15-20 minutes. Reduce heat, add ½ cup water and cook covered until the lamb is tender.

○ Blanch the Madras onions, toss them in a little butter and keep aside.

○ Remove the lid, add spices and Madras onions; cook covered for 5 minutes. Uncover, add cream and mix well. Serve hot garnished with green coriander and ginger.

Shammi Kebabs

Shallow-fried lamb patties

Ingredients serves: 4

Lamb, boneless ~ 500 gm
Bengal gram (*chana dal*), washed
~ 3 tbsp / 75 gm
Water ~ 7½ cups / 1.5 lt
Turmeric (*haldi*) powder ~ ½ tsp
For the marinade:
Ginger (*adrak*) paste ~ 1 tsp / 6 gm
Garlic (*lasan*) paste ~ 1 tsp / 6 gm
Red chilli powder ~ 1½ tsp / 3 gm
Garam masala (see p. 24)
~ 1 tsp / 2 gm
Green cardamom (*choti elaichi*)
powder ~ ½ tsp

Mace (*javitri*) powder
~ ½ tsp
Green chillies, chopped ~ 3
Corn oil ~ 4 tbsp / 60 ml
Green coriander (*hara dhaniya*),
finely chopped ~ 3 tbsp / 12 gm

Refined oil for shallow frying
Onion, sliced ~ 1
Yoghurt (*dahi*) ~ 2 tbsp / 60 gm
Green chillies, finely chopped ~ 2
Egg, beaten ~ 1
Salt ~ 1½ tsp / 6 gm

Method

○ Boil Bengal gram with 2½ cups water in a heavy-bottomed pan.
Add turmeric powder and cook for about 20 minutes or till the
water is absorbed and the Bengal gram is soft enough to be mashed
to a paste in a food processor.

○ For the marinade, mix all the ingredients together and rub into
the lamb.

○ Heat the oil in a pan; add onion and sauté till golden brown. Add
lamb and stir-fry for a few minutes. Pour in the remaining water
and lower heat. Cook covered till the water is absorbed and the
lamb is soft enough to be ground.

○ Grind the lamb for about 1-2 minutes and transfer in a bowl.

- Add yoghurt, mashed Bengal gram, and green chillies; mix well. Add egg and salt; mix again.
- Divide the mixture equally into 12 portions. Shape each into flat rounds.
- Heat the oil in a pan; shallow-fry 2-3 kebab at a time turning them gently, till dark brown. Remove with a slotted spoon and drain the excess oil on absorbent kitchen paper towels.
- Serve hot accompanied with mint chutney (see p. 107) and garnished with lemon wedges and onion rings.

The Six P's

Kundan Lal's secret of success was his six P's formula. He believed that in his trade the six P's: Product, Price, Promotion, Place, Personalized service, and People were all important.

Delegates of honourary magistrates of Commonwealth on their arrival to India, seen with son of Kundan Lal Gujral, Nand Lal (standing first from left).

Kundan Lal Gujral with son, Nand Lal, daughter-in-law, Rupa, and friends, Mr Dhupia and Dharamvira at a reception in Moti Mahal.

Seekh Kebabs

Skewered lamb kebabs

Ingredients serves: 4

Minced lamb (*keema*) ~ 500 gm
Egg, beaten ~ 1
Onion, finely chopped ~ 1
Green chilies, finely chopped ~ 2
Red chilli powder ~ 5 tsp / 10 gm
Ginger (*adrak*), chopped
~ 1 tsp / 6 gm

Garam masala (see p. 24)
~ 5 tsp / 10 gm
Salt to taste
Green coriander (*hara dhaniya*),
chopped ~ 2 tbsp / 8 gm
Lemon (*nimbu*), cut into
wedges ~ 1

Method

○ Combine all the ingredients (except the last two) in a bowl; mix thoroughly.

○ Divide the mixture equally into 16 balls. Skewer each ball and with wet hands make 2"-long kebabs.

○ Put the skewers in the tandoor and cook for about 5-6 minutes.

○ Take the skewers out and baste with some oil. Then put it back in the tandoor for about 5-6 minutes. Repeat till all the kebabs are done.

○ Arrange the kebabs on a platter and garnish with green coriander and lemon wedges

Barra Kebabs

Lamb chops grilled in a tandoor

Ingredients   serves: 4

Lamb chops, leg pieces ~ 1 kg

For the marinade:

Salt to taste

Red chilli powder ~ 1 tbsp

Black cumin (*shah jeera*)

powder ~ 3 tbsp

Garam masala (see p. 24)

~ 8 tsp / 16 gm

Garlic (*lasan*) paste ~ 3 tbsp / 54 gm

Ginger (*adrak*) paste

~ 3 tbsp / 54 gm

Kachri (tenderizer) ~ 5 tsp / 25 gm

Raw papaya paste

~ 5 tsp / 25 gm

Lemon (*nimbu*) juice

~ 5 tbsp / 75 ml

Yoghurt (*dahi*) ~ ½ cup / 100 gm

Refined oil for basting

Method

○ For the marinade, mix all the ingredients together (except the oil) and rub into the lamb pieces. Keep overnight or for 8 hours.

○ Skewer the pieces 1" apart and roast on a slow fire, in a tandoor or charcoal grill for 15 minutes or till half done.

○ Remove the skewers and hang them for 15 minutes for the excess marinade to drip off; baste with oil.

○ Roast again for 15 minutes more or till tender.

○ Arrange on a platter and garnish with green coriander and lemon wedges.

○ Serve with mint chutney (see p. 107).

Badaam Parsinda Gosht

Lamb cooked semi-dry with almonds

Ingredients   serves: 4

Parsindas, cut out of loin or shoulder,
cut into 2" x 3" pieces ¼" thick
~ 15 / 500 gm
Salt ~ ½ tsp
Red chilli powder ~ 2 tsp / 4 gm
Garam masala (see p. 24) ~ ½ tsp
For the stuffing:
Ghee ~ 2 tbsp / 30 gm
Onions, finely chopped ~ 2
Ginger (*adrak*), chopped
~ 2 tsp / 12 gm
Almonds (*badaam*), blanched,
chopped ~ 2 tbsp / 30 gm
Pistachios (*pista*), roughly chopped
~ 2 tbsp / 30 gm
Cashew nuts (*kaju*), roughly
chopped ~ 2 tbsp / 30 gm
Green chillies, finely
chopped ~ 50 gm
For the coating:
Red chilli powder ~ ¼ tsp

Refined flour (*maida*) ~ 2 tbsp / 20 gm
Salt ~ ¼ tsp
Garam masala ~ ½ tsp
For the gravy:
Ghee ~ 1 cup / 200 gm
Onions, grated ~ ⅔ cup / 100 gm
Water ~ 2½ cups / 500 ml
Red chilli powder ~ 1 tsp / 2 gm
Turmeric (*haldi*) powder ~ ½ tsp
Salt ~ 1 tsp / 4 gm
Coriander (*dhaniya*) seeds, ground
~ 2 tsp / 4 gm
Yoghurt (*dahi*), whisked
~ 1½ cups / 250 gm
Ginger, chopped ~ 1 tbsp / 24 gm
Garlic (*lasan*) cloves ~ 8
Garam masala ~ 1 tsp / 2 gm
Green coriander (*hara dhaniya*),
chopped ~ 1 tbsp / 4 gm
Black cumin (*shah jeera*)
seeds, roasted, ground ~ 1 tsp / 2 gm

Method

○ For the stuffing, heat the ghee in a wok *(kadhai)*; add onions and
sauté till golden brown. Add ginger, almonds, pistachios, cashew
nuts, green chillies, and salt. Stir-fry for about 5 minutes. Remove
from heat and divide the mixture into 15 equal parts.

- Dust the *parsindas* with seasoning made of salt, red chilli powder, and garam masala.
- Place 1 part of stuffing over each *parsinda* and roll it up. Tie a piece of thread to seal the filling inside.
- Roll the *parsindas* over a mixture of red chilli powder, flour, salt, and garam masala.
- Heat the ghee in a wok *(kadhai)*; add the stuffed *parsindas* and fry till golden brown. Remove with a slotted spoon and drain the excess oil on absorbent paper towels.
- For the gravy, heat the ghee and fry onions till brown. Add 2 tbsp water and fry till it evaporates. Add red chilli powder and 1 tbsp water and fry till it evaporates again.
- Add turmeric powder, salt, coriander seeds, and yoghurt; mix well. Mix in the stuffed *parsindas*. Add ginger and garlic; stir for a few minutes. Add garam masala and the remaining water.
- Cook the *parsindas* covered on low heat till tender, add more water if required. Cook till the mixture is almost dry.
- Serve hot garnished with green coriander and sprinkled with black cumin seeds.

Fish Kebabs

Shallow-fried fish patties

Fish ~ 500 gm

Ginger (*adrak*) paste ~ 1 tsp / 6 gm

Garlic (*lasan*) paste ~ 1 tsp / 6 gm

Lemon (*nimbu*) juice ~ 1 tsp / 5 ml

Garam masala (see p. 24) ~ ½ tsp

Salt to taste

Mint (*pudina*) leaves, chopped
~ 2 tbsp / 8 gm

Green chillies, chopped ~ 2-3

Gram flour (*besan*) or cornflour
~ 2 tbsp / 40 gm

Refined oil for shallow frying

Method

○ Place the fish in a colander kept over a pan of boiling water or steam in a microwave for 4-5 minutes, covered, till the fish is tender. Remove the bones and skin.

○ Add all the ingredients except oil and mix well.

○ Divide the mixture equally into lemon-sized portions. Flatten each into the shape of kebabs and shallow-fry on a non-stick griddle (*tawa*) till golden brown. Remove and drain the excess oil on absorbent paper towels.

○ Serve hot with mint chutney (see p. 107) and lemon wedges.

Fish Tikka

Grilled fish cubes

Fish (sole), cut into cubes ~ 500 gm

Lemon (*nimbu*) juice

~ 1 tbsp / 15 ml

For the first marinade:

Lemon juice ~ 2 tbsp / 30 ml

Salt to taste

Red chilli powder ~ 1 tsp / 2 gm

For the second marinade:

Ginger (*adrak*) paste ~ 1 tsp / 6 gm

Garlic (*lasan*) paste ~ 2 tsp / 12 gm

Yoghurt (*dahi*) ~ 3 tbsp / 90 gm

Carom seeds (*ajwain*) ~ ½ tsp

Dry fenugreek leaves (*kasoori methi*)

~ 1 tsp / ½ gm

Red colour ~ 2 drops

Gram flour (*besan*) ~ 2 tbsp / 20 gm

Refined oil for basting

Chaat masala (see p. 25)

~ 1 tsp / 2 gm

Method

○ Rub the fish with lemon juice, wash and pat dry.

○ For the first marinade, mix all the ingredients and rub into the fish. Keep aside for 30 minutes.

○ For the second marinade, mix all the ingredients together and rub into the fish. Add gram flour and keep aside for another 30 minutes.

○ Grill in a medium-hot oven for 10 minutes. Then remove and baste with oil; return to the oven and grill again for about 10 minutes or till done.

○ Arrange on a platter, sprinkle some *chaat* masala and serve with mint chutney (see p. 107).

Khatti Machchi

Tangy fish

Ingredients serves: 4

Fish, cut into 2" fillets
~ 8-9 / 500 gm
Water ~ 1 cup / 200 ml
Lemon (*nimbu*) juice
~ 4 tbsp / 60 ml
Black pepper (*kali mirch*) powder
~ 1½ tsp / 3 gm
Salt ~ 1 tsp / 4 gm
Cumin (*jeera*) powder
~ 1 tsp / 1½ gm

Carom (*ajwain*) seeds or oregano
powder ~ ½ tsp
Garlic (*lasan*) cloves, finely
chopped ~ 6-7
Onion, large, sliced ~ 1
Capsicum (*Shimla mirch*), sliced
(green or yellow or red or a mixture
of all 3) ~ 2
Cornflour, dissolved in 1 tbsp water
~ 1 tsp / 2 gm

Method

○ In a large, non-stick pan, add water, lemon juice, black pepper, salt, cumin powder, carom seeds, garlic, and onion. Cook covered on medium heat for 3-4 minutes or till the onion is tender. Add fish and cook covered on medium heat for 10 minutes or till soft.

○ Remove the fish into a serving dish with a slotted spoon.

○ Add capsicum and cook for 1-2 minutes or till tender but crisp.

○ Add cornflour paste and after one boil pour the sauce over the fish and serve hot.

Machchi Punjabi Curry

Punjabi fish curry

Ingredients serves: 4

Fish, boneless, fillets ~ 12
Refined oil ~ 2 tbsp / 30 ml
Mustard seeds (*rai*) ~ 1 tsp / 3 gm
Garlic (*lasan*), cloves, chopped ~ 8
Ginger (*adrak*), 1" piece, cut into
small pieces ~ 1
Green chilies, slit lengthwise,
deseeded, cut into small
pieces ~ 6

Onions, grated ~ ¾ cup / 150 gm
Turmeric (*haldi*) powder ~ ½ tsp
Curry leaves (*kadhi patta*) ~ 2-3
Tomatoes, puréed, strained ~ 3
Salt to taste
Vinegar (*sirka*) ~ 1 tbsp / 15 ml
Cream, fresh ~ 2 tbsp / 40 ml
Green coriander (*hara dhaniya*),
chopped ~ 1 tbsp / 4 gm

Method

○ Heat the oil in a pan; add mustard seeds. Stir over medium heat until they begin to splutter. Add garlic and ginger; sauté for a minute. Add green chillies and onions; sauté until brown.

○ Add turmeric powder, curry leaves, and tomatoes. Fry for 2-3 minutes. Add fish, salt, and vinegar.

○ Lower heat and cook covered for a few minutes till the fish is tender.

○ Stir only once or twice and very gently to make sure that the fillets do not break. Taste and adjust the seasoning. Stir in the cream gently.

○ Serve garnished with green coriander and accompanied with rice.

Sharabi Jhinga

Tandoori prawns marinated in whisky

Ingredients   serves: 4

Prawns, king-sized ~ 12
Whisky ~ 3 tbsp / 45 ml
For the marinade:
Ginger (*adrak*) paste
~ 3 tbsp / 54 gm
Garlic (*lasan*) paste
~ 3 tbsp / 54 gm
Lemon (*nimbu*) juice
~ 6 tbsp / 90 ml
Salt to taste
Chick pea (*kabuli chana*) flour
~ 3 tbsp / 30 gm

Carom (*ajwain*) seeds
~ 1 tsp / 1½ gm
Yoghurt (*dahi*) ~ 2½ cups / 500 gm
Red chilli powder ~ 2 tsp / 4 gm
Garam masala (see p. 24)
~ 2 tsp / 4 gm
Turmeric (*haldi*) powder
~ 1 tsp / 2 gm
Butter for basting
Chaat masala (see p. 25)
~ 2 tsp / 4 gm
Lemon juice ~ 2 tbsp / 30 ml

Method

○ Marinate the prawns with whisky for 1 hour.

○ For the marinade, mix all the ingredients together (except the last 3) and rub into the prawns. Marinate for another 2 hours.

○ Skewer the prawns and cook in a tandoor for about 10 minutes or till half done.

○ Remove and hang the skewer for 10 minutes, then return to the tandoor again and cook for 5 minutes more.

○ Baste with butter and then return to the tandoor for 3 more minutes.

○ Remove and arrange them on a serving dish and sprinkle with *chaat* masala and lemon juice.

Tamatar Jhinga

Prawns in tomato cream sauce

Ingredients serves: 4

Prawns, peeled, washed ~ 500 gm

For the sauce:

Tomato purée ~ 5 tbsp / 75 ml

Salt ~ ¾ tsp

Sugar ~ ¼ tsp

Garam masala (see p. 24)
~ 1 tsp / 2 gm

Cumin (*jeera*) seeds, roasted,
ground ~ ½ tsp

Red chilli powder ~ ½ tsp

Green coriander (*hara dhaniya*),
chopped ~ 3 tbsp / 12 gm

Green chilli, finely
chopped ~ 1

Lemon (*nimbu*) juice
~ 1 tbsp / 15 ml

Single cream ~ 1 cup / 200 ml

Refined oil ~ 3 tbsp / 45 ml

Black mustard (*rai*) seeds
~ 1 tsp / 3 gm

Garlic (*lasan*) cloves, finely
chopped ~ 3

Curry leaves (*kadhi patta*) ~ 10-15

Method

○ For the sauce, put all the ingredients in a bowl, mix well.

○ Gradually stir in the cream and keep aside.

○ Heat the oil in a wok *(kadhai)*; add mustard seeds. When they start popping, add garlic and curry leaves; sauté until garlic turns medium brown.

○ Add the prawns and stir until they are opaque most of the way through. Add the sauce. Reduce the flame to medium and heat the sauce through until it begins to simmer.

○ Remove the wok from the heat and serve with rice.

VEGETARIAN

Tandoori Gobi

Tandoori cauliflower garnished with onion rings

Ingredients   serves: 4

Cauliflower (*phool gobi*)
~ 3 / 300 gm each
For the marinade:
Yoghurt (*dahi*), hung for 25 minutes
~ 1½ cups / 300 gm
Ginger (*adrak*) paste
~ 2 tbsp / 36 gm
Garlic (*lasan*) paste ~ 1 tbsp / 18 gm
Salt to taste
Turmeric (*haldi*) powder ~ ½ tsp
Red chilli powder ~ 1 tsp / 2 gm
Garam masala (see p. 24)
~ 1½ tsp / 3 gm

Coriander (*dhaniya*) powder ~ ½ tsp
Chaat masala (see p. 25)
~ 1 tsp / 2 gm
For the topping:
Refined oil ~ 3 tbsp / 45 ml
Onions, cut into rings ~ 3-4
Tomato purée ~ ¼ cup / 50 ml
Garam masala ~ 1 tsp / 2 gm
Chaat masala ~ ½ tsp
Salt to taste
Green coriander (*hara dhaniya*),
finely chopped
~ 4-5 tbsp / 16-20 gm

Method

○ Boil 5-6 cups of water in a pan with 2 tsp salt. Add cauliflower and cook till barely tender. Remove from water and keep aside to dry.

○ For the marinade, mix all the ingredients and rub into the cauliflower covering all the florets. Keep aside for 45 minutes.

○ Preheat the oven at 200°C / 400°F and grill the cauliflower till golden brown and crisp.

○ For the topping, heat the oil in a pan; add onion rings and tomato purée. When the onions are light brown, add garam masala, *chaat* masala, and salt.

○ Arrange the cauliflower on a platter, garnish with green coriander and spread the topping; serve hot.

Tandoori Arbi

Grilled colocasia

Ingredients serves: 4

Colocasia (*arbi*) ~ 500 gm

Yoghurt (*dahi*), hung, drained for 25

minutes ~ 1 cup / 200 gm

Refined oil ~ 5 tbsp / 75 ml

Carom seeds (*ajwain*)

~ 1 tsp / 3 gm

Salt to taste

Chaat masala (see p. 25)

~ 1 tsp / 2 gm

Red chilli powder ~ ½ tsp

Onions, sliced ~ 2

Coriander (*dhaniya*) powder

~ 1 tsp / 2 gm

Mango powder (*amchur*) ~ ½ tsp

Salt to taste

Garam masala (see p. 24) ~ ½ tsp

Lemon (*nimbu*) juice

~ 1 tsp / 5 ml

Method

○ Boil the colocasia in a pressure cooker for 10-15 minutes or till one whistle. Remove from heat and gently release the pressure. When cool enough to handle, peel and cut the colocasia into pieces. Flatten each piece slightly.

○ Mix yoghurt with1 tbsp oil, carom seeds, salt, chaat masala, and red chilli powder. Rub this into the colocasia and keep aside for 30 minutes.

○ Heat the oven at 190°C / 375°F, brush the rack with some oil. Place the colocasia in the oven and grill for 25 minutes or till the yoghurt dries completely.

○ Heat the remaining oil in a pan. Reduce heat, add onions and sauté till golden brown. Add coriander powder, mango powder, salt, garam masala, and grilled colocasia. Stir-fry for a few minutes. Add lemon juice and mix well.

○ Serve hot with lemon wedges and onion rings.

Tandoori Aloo

Grilled potatoes stuffed with cottage cheese

Ingredients serves: 4

Potatoes, medium-sized, washed, parboiled, peeled, halved ~ 1 kg

For the stuffing:

Cottage cheese (*paneer*), crumbled ~ 2 tbsp /30 gm

Salt to taste

Cashew nuts (*kaju*) ~ 3 tbsp / 45 gm

Raisins (*kishmish*) ~ 3 tbsp / 30 gm

Green chillies, chopped ~ 2-3

White pepper (*safed mirch*) powder ~ 2 tsp / 4 gm

Cream, fresh ~ 1 tbsp / 20 ml

Gram flour (*besan*) ~ 1 cup / 100 gm

Red chilli (*degi mirch*) powder ~ 1 tsp / 2 gm

Lemon (*nimbu*) juice ~ 1 tbsp / 15 ml

Chaat masala (see p. 25) ~ 2 tsp / 4 gm

Method

- Scoop the potatoes from the centre with a spoon leaving a hollow behind.
- For the stuffing, mix all the ingredients together in a bowl.
- Stuff the filling in the hollow potatoes.
- In a bowl, add gram flour, red chilli powder, 1 tsp lemon juice, and a little water to make a smooth paste. Rub this paste on the potato shells and keep aside for 15 minutes.
- Place the marinated potatoes on the grill rack and grill in a hot oven at 200°C / 400°F till the potatoes are crisp and golden brown.
- Serve hot sprinkled with *chaat* masala.

Jimikand Ke Kebabs

Yam kebabs

Ingredients serves: 4

Yam (*jimikand*), washed,
peeled ~ 1½ kg
Salt ~ 1½ tsp / 6 gm
Ginger (*adrak*), finely chopped
~ 1 tsp / 10 gm
White pepper (*safed mirch*) powder
~ 2 tsp / 4 gm
Breadcrumbs ~ ½ cup / 60 gm

Red chilli (*degi mirch*) powder
~ 2 tsp / 4 gm
Green coriander (*hara dhaniya*),
chopped ~ 1 tsp
Green chillies, finely chopped ~ 2
Chaat masala (see p. 25)
~ 2 tsp / 4 gm
Refined oil ~ ¾ cup / 150 ml

Method

○ Boil the water in a pan, add yam and cook till tender. Remove and squeeze out the excess water. Then grate finely.

○ Mix the remaining ingredients except the oil with the grated yam. Divide the mixture equally into 10 portions. Shape them into ovals.

○ Heat the oil in a wok (*kadhai*); shallow fry the kebabs, a few at a time, on medium heat, till crisp and golden brown. Remove with a slotted spoon and drain the excess oil on absorbent paper towels.

○ Serve hot with mint chutney (see p. 107).

Seekh-e-Subz

Skewered vegetable kebabs

Ingredients serves: 4

Potatoes, medium-sized, boiled,
peeled, mashed ~ 4
Beans (*sem*), finely chopped
~ ½ cup
Carrots (*gajar*) ~ ½ cup
Cottage cheese (*paneer*),
crumbled ~ ½ cup
Cashew nuts (*kaju*), ground
~ 4 tbsp / 60 gm
Cauliflower (*phool gobi*) ~ 125 gm
Ginger (*adrak*), chopped
~ 2 tsp / 12 gm

Onions, minced
~ ¼ cup / 30 gm
Green chillies, minced ~ 2
Red chilli (*degi mirch*) powder
~ 2 tsp / 4 gm
Cumin (*jeera*) powder
~ 1 tsp / 2 gm
Green coriander (*hara dhaniya*),
minced ~ 2 tbsp / 8 gm
Salt to taste
Breadcrumbs ~ 2 tbsp / 30 gm
Refined oil for basting

Method

○ Mix all the ingredients together with the boiled potatoes except the oil and knead to a stiff dough. Keep aside for 25 minutes.

○ With moist hands, spread the mixture along the skewers into a shape of a kebab.

○ Cook in a tandoor or oven for 10 minutes. Remove and baste with oil and cook for 5 more minutes. Remove from the skewers and repeat till all the dough is used up.

○ Serve hot with mint chutney (see p. 107).

Film star Prem Chopra with Kundan Lal and friends.

The leading star of yesteryears, Nargis, with Kundan Lal Gujral and friends at the launch of her all time classic movie *Mother India*.

Paneer Ke Kebabs

Cottage cheese kebabs

Ingredients serves: 4

Cottage cheese (*paneer*),
finely grated ~ 1 kg
Red chilli (*degi mirch*)
powder ~ 2 tsp / 4 gm
Garam masala (see p. 24)
~ 3 tsp / 6 gm
Ginger (*adrak*), chopped
~ 2 tsp / 12 gm
Green chillies, finely chopped ~ 3
Lemon (*nimbu*) juice ~ 1 tbsp / 15 ml

Salt to taste
White pepper (*safed mirch*)
powder ~ 2 tsp / 4 gm
Cornflour
(*makki ka atta*) ~ 2 tbsp / 16 gm
Refined oil for basting
Green coriander (*hara dhaniya*),
chopped for garnishing
Lemons (*nimbu*), cut into
wedges ~ 2

Method

○ Mix all the ingredients (except the last three) adding cornflour in the end.

○ Divide the mixture equally into 12 portions.

○ With moist hands, spread the mixture on the skewers evenly.

○ Roast in an oven or tandoor for 5-6 minutes and then remove and baste with oil. Cook for another 2-3 minutes or till golden brown.

○ Remove from the skewers and garnish with green coriander and lemon wedges.

○ Serve with mint chutney (see p. 107).

Mirchi Ka Salan

Green chilli curry

Ingredients serves: 4

Green chillies ~ 10

Tamarind (*imli*) ~ 8 tbsp / 50 gm

Water ~ 4¼ cups / 850 ml

Grind together:

Sesame (*til*) seeds ~ 3 tbsp / 15 gm

Coconut (*nariyal*), dessicated

~ 2 tsp / 4 gm

Coriander (*dhaniya*) seeds ~ 2 tsp / 4 gm

Cumin (*jeera*) powder ~ 2 tsp / 4 gm

Salt ~ 1 tsp / 4 gm

Ginger (*adrak*) paste ~ 1½ tsp / 9 gm

Garlic (*lasan*) paste ~ 1 tsp / 6 gm

Turmeric (*haldi*) powder ~ ½ tsp

Lemon (*nimbu*) juice ~ 1 tsp / 6 ml

Salad oil ~ 5 tbsp / 75 ml

Curry leaves (*kadhi patta*) ~ 3-4

Onion seeds (*kalonji*) ~ ½ tsp / 2 gm

Mustard seeds (*rai*) ~ ¼ tsp

Onions, finely chopped ~ 3

Cashew nut (*kaju*) paste,

ground with 2 tbsp milk

~ 4 tsp / 40 gm

Cream, fresh ~ 2 tbsp / 40 ml

Green coriander (*hara dhaniya*),

chopped for garnishing

Method

○ Soak tamarind in a bowl with 1¾ cups hot water. Mash with a fork and keep aside for 1 hour.

○ Grind sesame seeds and coconut together for 30 seconds. Then add the remaining ingredients. Grind for 30 seconds.

○ Heat the oil in a pan; fry green chillies for about 1½ minutes. Remove and keep aside. In the same oil, add curry leaves, onion seeds, and mustard seeds; sauté till they crackle. Add onions and the ground paste; sauté for 2 minutes. Add cashew nut paste.

○ Pour the remaining water in the pan and mix well. Strain the tamarind juice and stir in the pan. Add fried green chillies and cook for 5 minutes. Stir in the cream. Serve garnished with green coriander.

Tandoori Vegetables

Ingredients   serves: 4

Capsicum (*Shimla mirch*),
cut into large cubes ~ 2
Tomatoes, leave the small ones
whole, large ones cut
into 8 pieces, pulp
removed ~ 5 small or 2 large
Mushrooms, stems removed ~ 10
Broccoli, cut into
medium-sized florets ~ 250 gm
Baby corns, parboiled ~ 100 gm
Onions, small, cut into 4 pieces ~ 2

For the marinade:
Yoghurt (*dahi*), hung for
10 minutes ~ 1 cup / 200 gm
Cream, double ~ 2 tbsp / 40 ml
Black salt (*kala namak*) ~ ½ tsp
Garam masala (see p. 24) ~ ½ tsp
Red chilli (*degi mirch*) powder ~ ½ tsp
Salt ~ ¾ tsp / 3 gm

Olive oil for basting
Chaat masala (see p. 25) ~ 2 tsp / 4 gm

Method

○ For the marinade, mix all the ingredients in a bowl and rub into the vegetables. Marinate for 30 minutes.

○ Skewer the vegetables and grill in a tandoor or in a preheated oven (200°C / 400°F) for about 10 minutes. Remove and baste with olive oil. Cook for 5 more minutes.

○ Arrange on a sizzler and sprinkle some chaat masala on the vegetables. Serve with mint chutney (see p. 107).

Kadhai Khumb

Mushrooms cooked in a wok

Ingredients serves: 4

Mushrooms, washed, halved ~ 250 gm
Refined oil ~ 5 tbsp / 75 ml
Coriander (*dhaniya*) seeds ~ 1 tsp / 2 gm
Ginger (*adrak*) paste ~ 1 tbsp / 18 gm
Garlic (*lasan*) paste ~ 1 tbsp / 18 gm
Dry red chillies (*sookhi lal mirch*) ~ 1-2
Onions, finely chopped ~ 2
Tomato purée ~ ½ cup / 100 ml
Salt to taste
Garam masala (see p. 24) ~ 1 tsp / 2 gm

Cumin (*jeera*) powder ~ 1 tsp / 1½ gm
Red chilli (*degi mirch*) powder ~ 1 tsp / 2 gm
Chaat masala (see p. 25) ~ 1 tsp / 2 gm
Capsicum (*Shimla mirch*), large ~ 1
Tomatoes, chopped ~ 1
Cream ~ 1 tbsp / 20 ml
Green coriander (*hara dhaniya*), chopped ~ 3 tbsp / 12 gm

Method

o Heat the oil in a wok *(kadhai)*; add mushrooms and sauté on low heat till golden brown. Remove mushrooms with a slotted spoon and drain the excess oil on absorbent paper towels.

o In the same oil, add coriander seeds; sauté till light brown. Add ginger-garlic paste, dry red chillies, and onions. Sauté till light brown.

o Add tomato purée and stir till the oil separates. Add salt, garam masala, cumin powder, red chilli powder, and *chaat* masala; mix well.

o Add capsicum and tomatoes. Stir well adding ¼ cup water. Add mushrooms and stir for 2-3 minutes.

o Mix in cream and serve hot garnished with green coriander.

Kadhai Paneer

Cottage cheese cooked in a wok

Ingredients   serves: 4

Cottage cheese (*paneer*),
cut into fingers ~ 500 gm
Refined oil ~ ½ cup / 100 ml
Ginger (*adrak*) paste ~ 1 tbsp / 18 gm
Garlic (*lasan*) paste ~ 1 tbsp / 18 gm
Onions, chopped ~ ¼ cup / 30 gm
Tomatoes, chopped ~ ½ cup / 250 gm
Coriander (*dhaniya*)
powder ~ 1 tsp / 1½ gm
Garam masala (see p. 24) ~ 2 tsp / 4 gm
Salt to taste

Dry fenugreek leaves
(*kasoori methi*) ~ 1 tsp / 1½ gm
Tomato purée ~ 1 cup / 200 ml
Capsicum (*Shimla mirch*),
julienned ~ 30 gm
Butter ~ 1 tbsp / 20 gm
Cream ~ 2 tbsp / 40 ml
Green coriander (*hara dhaniya*),
chopped ~ 1 tbsp / 4 gm
Green chillies,
slit into half ~ 2

Method

o   Heat the oil in a pan; add ginger-garlic paste and sauté till golden brown. Add onions and sauté for about 2 minutes.

o   Add tomatoes and cook till the oil separates. Add coriander powder, garam masala, salt, and dry fenugreek leaves. Stir in the tomato purée; cook for a few minutes.

o   Add capsicum and cottage cheese; mix well. Stir in butter and cream and cook for about a minute.

o   Serve hot garnished with green coriander and green chillies.

Bharwan Dum Aloo

Stuffed potatoes in tomato curry

Ingredients serves: 4

Potatoes, medium ~ 8
Refined oil for frying
For the stuffing:
Refined oil ~ ½ cup / 100 ml
Cumin (*jeera*) seeds
~ 2 tsp / 4 gm
Onions, chopped ~ 2
Black cardamom (*badi elaichi*)
pods, pounded ~ 2
Raisins (*kishmish*) ~ 5 tbsp / 50 gm
Cashew nuts (*kaju*) ~ 5 tbsp / 50 gm
Cottage cheese (*paneer*) ~ 50 gm
Salt to taste
For the curry:
Onions, chopped ~ ½ cup / 60 gm
Ginger-garlic (*adrak-lasan*)
paste ~ 3 tbsp / 54 gm

Tomato purée ~ 1 cup / 200 ml
Yoghurt (*dahi*), whisked
~ 1½ cups / 300 gm
Aniseed (*saunf*) ~ 1 tsp / 2 gm
Mace (*javitri*) powder
~ 1½ tsp / 3 gm
Cumin (*jeera*) seeds ~ 1 tsp / 2 gm
Green cardamom (*choti
elaichi*) ~ 4
Cloves (*laung*) ~ 6
Red chilli (*degi mirch*) powder
~ 3 tsp / 6 gm
Cumin (*jeera*) powder ~ 3 tsp / 4½ gm
Coriander (*dhaniya*)
powder ~ 1 tbsp / 12 gm
Salt to taste
Cream, fresh ~ 3 tbsp / 60 ml

Method

○ Peel the potatoes and slice the tops. With a sharp knife scoop out the centre. Fry the shells to a golden brown and allow them to cool.

○ For the stuffing, heat the oil in wok *(kadhai)*; add cumin seeds and onions. Sauté till onions turn transparent. Add black cardamom powder, raisins, cashew nuts, cottage cheese, and salt.

Stir-fry for a few minutes, strain the oil and then keep the mixture aside.

- ○ Stuff the shells with this prepared mixture and keep aside.
- ○ For the curry, reheat the oil in the pan; add the onions and sauté till transparent. Add ginger-garlic paste and stir for 2 minutes. Add tomato purée, yoghurt, aniseed, mace powder, cumin seeds, green cardamom, cloves, red chilli powder, cumin powder, coriander powder, and salt. Stir-fry for 10 minutes.
- ○ Immerse the stuffed potatoes in the curry, cover the pan with a lid, seal with a dough and cook on low heat for 10 minutes.
- ○ Garnish with cream, stirring in gently, and serve hot with rice.

Dal Makhani

Rich creamy dal in a butter gravy

Ingredients   serves: 4

Black gram (*urad dal*),
whole ~ 3¹/₃ cups / 500 gm
Kidney beans (*rajma*)
~ 1¾ cups / 250 gm
Bengal gram (*chana dal*)
~ 1¾ cups / 250 gm
Milk ~ 5 cups / 1 lt

Tomato purée ~ 5 cups / 1 lt
Salt to taste
Red chilli powder ~ 25 gm
Cumin (*jeera*) powder ~ 25 gm
Garam masala (see p. 24) ~ 25 gm
Butter ~ 1 kg
Cream ~ 2½ cups / 500 ml

Method

○ Pick and clean the black gram, kidney beans, and Bengal gram. Add salt and rub the mixture with both hands and then rinse with water. Soak the mixture in water, overnight.

○ Take a heavy-based utensil, add the drained dal mixture and double the quantity of water; cook over low heat. Stir the mixture vigorously enough to mash it. Once it thickens, add milk and cook till the milk is absorbed completely.

○ Add tomato purée and all the spices. Cook till the grams and beans are tender (for about half an hour). Add butter and cook for another 10 minutes.

○ Add cream and mix well by stirring continuously.

○ Serve hot.

Navrattan Korma

Mixed vegetable delight

Ingredients   serves: 4

Carrots (*gajar*) ~ 1 cup

French beans ~ ²/₃ cup

Green peas (*hara muttar*) ~ 1 cup

Mushrooms ~ 1 cup

Potatoes, diced ~ 1 cup

Onions, chopped ~ ½ cup / 60 gm

Cauliflower (*phool gobi*),
cut into small florets ~ 1 cup

Green chillies, finely chopped ~ 2

Cottage cheese (*paneer*) ~ 50 gm

Refined oil ~ ¼ cup / 50 ml

Cloves (*laung*) ~ 10

Cinnamon (*dalchini*), 1" sticks ~ 2

Bay leaf (*tej patta*) ~ 1

Cumin (*jeera*) seeds ~ 1 tsp / 2 gm

Green cardamom
(*choti elaichi*) ~ 10

Ginger (*adrak*) paste ~ 2 tbsp / 36 gm

Garlic (*lasan*) paste ~ 2 tbsp / 36 gm

Cashew nut
(*kaju*) paste ~ ½ cup / 100 gm

Yoghurt (*dahi*) ~ 1 cup / 200 gm

Salt to taste

White pepper (*safed mirch*)
powder ~ 2 tsp / 4 gm

Butter ~ 1 tbsp / 20 gm

Cream ~ 3 tbsp / 60 ml

Green coriander
(*hara dhaniya*) ~ 3 tsp / 15 gm

Ginger (*adrak*),
julienned ~ 1 tsp / 5 gm

Cashew nuts (*kaju*) ~ 8

Almonds (*badaam*) ~ 8

Raisins (*kishmish*) ~ 8

Method

○ Parboil the vegetables and keep aside.

○ Heat the oil in a pan; add cloves, cinnamon sticks, bay leaf, cumin seeds, and green cardamom; sauté till light brown.

○ Add ginger, garlic, and cashew nut pastes. Cook until the oil separates from the mixture.

- Add yoghurt; mix well and cook on low heat. Add parboiled vegetables, cottage cheese, salt, and white pepper powder. Cook covered on low heat for 6-7 minutes.
- Add butter and stir for 2 minutes. Then add cream and stir for another 2 minutes.
- Transfer into a serving bowl and serve garnished with green coriander, ginger, and dry fruits.

Why Dal Makhani?

It should have been named tandoori dal makhani. *In those days, in the absence of pressure cookers all gravy items were cooked on a slow fire and thus took a long time to cook. In order to save time and hence waste energy in stirring, Kundan Lal started putting dal soaked in water overnight on the tandoor, so that by morning the dal was soft and partially cooked. To this he added the magical butter sauce and dollops of cream to give us the famous Moti Mahal dal which, till date, has not been duplicated by anyone.*

ACCOMPANIMENTS

Subz Pulao

Vegetable pilaf

Ingredients   serves: 4

Basmati rice, washed, soaked
for 30 minutes ~ 1 cup / 200 gm
Carrot (*gajar*), chopped ~ 20 gm
Green peas (*hara muttar*) ~ 20 gm
Cauliflower (*phool gobi*),
cut into florets ~ 20 gm
Cottage cheese (*paneer*),
cubed ~ 20 gm
Refined oil ~ 6 tbsp / 90 ml
Cloves (*laung*) ~ 4
Cinnamon (*dalchini*)
1" stick ~ 1
Green cardamom
(*choti elaichi*) ~ 3
Bay leaf (*tej patta*) ~ 1
Black peppercorns
(*sabut kali mirch*) ~ 6
Black cumin (*shah jeera*)
seeds ~ 1 tsp / 2 gm
Onions, chopped ~ ½ cup / 60 gm

Ginger (*adrak*) ~ paste 1 tbsp / 18 gm
Red chilli (*degi mirch*) powder
~ 1½ tsp / 3 gm
White pepper (*safed mirch*)
powder ~ 1 tsp / 2 gm
Salt to taste
Water ~ 2½ cups / 500 ml
Green chillies, slit ~ 2
Onion, sliced, fried till golden brown
~ 2 tsp / 10 gm
Mace (*javitri*) powder ~ 1 tsp / 2 gm
Lemon (*nimbu*) juice ~ 1 tbsp / 15 ml
Ginger (*adrak*), julienned
~ 1 tsp / 3 gm
Cashew nuts (*kaju*),
fried till golden ~ 8
Green coriander (*hara dhaniya*),
chopped ~ 1 tsp
Cream ~ 2 tbsp / 40 ml
Vetivier (*kewda*) essence ~ 4 drops

Method

○   Heat the oil in a heavy-bottomed pan; add whole spices and
sauté until they begin to crackle. Add onions and stir-fry
till transparent.

- Add ginger paste, red chilli powder, white pepper powder, salt and all the vegetables. Cook for 4-5 minutes.
- Add the drained rice and water. Bring to the boil. Lower heat and cook covered till the rice is nearly done.
- Remove the lid and add green chillies, onion, mace powder, lemon juice, ginger, cashew nuts, green coriander, and cream. Seal the lid with a dough and cook for about 10 more minutes.
- Sprinkle vetivier essence and serve hot with mint raita.

Stress Buster

Once while my grandfather was teaching me how to cook, he told me, 'Cooking is like yoga as it enables me to release all my tensions and helps me to focus and concentrate better.'

Murgh Biryani

Chicken cooked with rice

Ingredients serves: 4

Basmati rice ~ 1 kg
Chicken, cut into pieces ~ 1 kg
For the marinade:
Yoghurt (*dahi*) ~ 1½ cups / 300 gm
Ginger-garlic (*adrak-lasan*)
paste ~ 3 tbsp / 54 gm
Salt to taste
Red chilli powder ~ 1 tbsp
Garam masala (see p. 24)
~ 1 tsp / 2 gm

Ghee ~ 1¼ cups / 250 gm
Bay leaves (*tej patta*) ~ 3

Green cardamom (*choti elaichi*) ~ 6
Black peppercorns
(*sabut kali mirch*) ~ 5
Cloves (*laung*) ~ 6
Cinnamon (*dalchini*), 1" stick ~ 1
Cumin (*jeera*) seeds ~ 2 tsp / 4 gm
Onions, sliced ~ 1¼ cups / 150 gm
Green coriander (*hara dhaniya*),
chopped ~ 2 tbsp / 8 gm
Chicken stock, boil some chicken
bones in water and strain ~ 20 cups
Milk ~ ½ cup / 100 ml
Saffron (*kesar*) ~ ½ tsp

Method

- For the marinade, mix all the ingredients and rub into the chicken.
- Heat about ¾ cup ghee in a pot *(handi)*; add whole spices and half the onions, sauté till golden brown. Add chicken and sauté till the water evaporates.
- Stir in the rest of the marinade and green coriander. Cook till the chicken pieces are tender.
- Boil the rice in the chicken stock.
- Heat a little ghee in a pan; fry the remaining onions till golden brown. Keep aside.

- Make a mixture of the remaining ghee, milk, and saffron by heating all together.
- In a pot arrange layers of chicken, rice, fried onions, and the saffron mixture. Repeat till the rice and chicken are over. Cover the pot with a lid and seal with the dough. Cook on low heat or bake in a medium-hot oven for about 10-15 minutes.
- Serve hot with mint *raita*.

The Love of His Life

Kundan Lal Gujral was one man who lived to perfect what he pursued. What he pursued were the two loves of his life—his love for people and his love for his restaurant. He was a legendary example of a perfect PR and a master inventor chef.

Gosht Biryani

Lamb cooked with rice

Ingredients serves: 4

Lamb ~ 750 gm
Papaya (*papita*), small, diced ~ 1
For the marinade:
Yoghurt (*dahi*), whisked
~1½ cups / 300 gm
Ginger (*adrak*) ~ paste1½ tsp / 9 gm
Garlic (*lasan*) paste ~ 1½ tsp / 9 gm
Red chilli powder ~ 1 tsp / 2 gm
Salt to taste
Green cardamom (*choti elaichi*)
powder ~ 1 tsp / 2 gm
Garam masala (see p. 24) ~ 2 tsp / 4 gm

Basmati rice ~ 600 gm

Water ~ 5 cups / 1 lt
Black cardamom
(*badi elaichi*) ~ 2
Cinnamon (*dalchini*), 1" stick ~ 1
Black cumin
(*shah jeera*) seeds ~ 1 tsp / 3 gm
Ghee ~ 6 tbsp / 90 gm
Onions, medium, sliced ~ 3
Green chillies ~ 3
Lemon (*nimbu*) juice ~ 4 tbsp / 60 ml
Saffron (*kesar*), dissolved in ¾ cup
milk ~ 2 tsp / 2 gm
Green coriander (*hara dhaniya*),
chopped ~ 2 tbsp / 8 gm

Method

○ Blend the papaya to a smooth paste. Rub it on the lamb pieces and leave for 30 minutes.

○ For the marinade, mix all the ingredients in a bowl and rub into the lamb. Marinate for 2 hours.

○ Wash the rice and meanwhile bring water to the boil in a pan with black cardamom, cinnamon stick, black cumin seeds, and 1 tsp salt.

○ Add rice to the boiling water and cook for 5-6 minutes. Once ¾ cooked, drain rice and keep aside.

Kundan Lal Gujral just before leaving for USSR with his *rakhi* sister, Dolly Arora (standing to his right) to open a branch of his restaurant at the International Trade Fair in Moscow after being invited by former USSR president Nikita Krushchev.

Kundan Lal Gujral with his son, Nand Lal, receiving the Worldwide Tourism Award in 1987, for tourist promotion in the restaurant category.

○ Heat the ghee in a heavy-bottomed pan; add onions and sauté till golden brown. Remove about 2 tbsp of onions and keep aside. Add lamb and stir for 5-6 minutes. Lower heat, add rice, top with reserved onions, green chillies, lemon juice, and saffron-milk mixture. Cover the pan with a lid and seal with dough; cook over low heat for about 45 minutes.

○ Check to see if the lamb is tender and then serve garnished with green coriander.

The Secret Masala

The special masala and the secret ingredients to make this masala were not revealed to anyone. Kundan Lal would personally supervise the grinding of these ingredients. He would put it in a plastic jar and keep it under the reception counter where he sat in the restaurant. Once the basic cooking had been done by the cooks, he would go to the kitchen and personally sprinkle the masala over the dishes. When I asked him the purpose of this exercise everyday, the reply I got was this keeps him close to his cooks and also ensures the alertness of the kitchen staff, as the boss could come at any time for the final touch!

Gatti Pulao

Moti Mahal Pulao

Ingredients serves: 4

Basmati rice, cleaned, washed,
soaked for 1 hour ~ 800 gm
Chicken, cut into 8 pieces ~ 750 gm
Minced lamb, parboiled
till done ~ 100 gm
Lamb, boneless, cut into small cubes,
parboiled till tender ~ 100 gm
Refined oil ~ ½ cup / 100 ml
Ginger-garlic (*adrak-lasan*)
paste ~ 2 tbsp / 36 gm
Salt ~ 1¹/₃ tsp / 5 gm
Water ~ ½ cup / 100 ml
Green cardamom (*choti elaichi*) ~ 8
Black cardamom (*badi elaichi*) ~ 4
Cloves (*laung*) ~ 8
Black peppercorns
(*sabut kali mirch*) ~ 4
Bay leaves (*tej patta*) ~ 4

Cinnamon (*dalchini*), 1" sticks ~ 4
Onions, chopped ~ 1½ cups / 180 gm
Garam masala (see p. 24)
~ 1 tsp / 2 gm
Red chilli powder ~ 1 tsp / 2 gm
Green chillies, slit ~ 4
Button mushrooms ~ 30 gm
French beans, chopped ~ 30 gm
Green peas (*hara muttar*) ~ 30 gm
Yoghurt (*dahi*), whisked
~ ½ cup / 100 gm
Chicken stock ~ 1½ cups / 300 ml
Egg, hard-boiled, cut into
half ~ 1
Tomato, cut into pieces ~ 1
Green coriander (*hara dhaniya*),
chopped ~ 2 tbsp / 8 gm
Vetivier (*kewda*) ~ 2 tsp / 10 ml

Method

○ Heat 2 tsp oil in a pan; add ginger-garlic paste and stir. Add chicken and sauté on medium heat; stir in salt and water and cook till water dries up. Keep aside.

○ Heat the remaining oil in a heavy-bottomed pan; add whole spices and sauté till they crackle. Add onions and sauté till light brown. Add garam masala and red chilli powder.

- Stir in green chillies, mushrooms, French beans, and green peas.
- Add the lamb pieces and sauté for a few minutes. Then add minced lamb and chicken, stir continuously.
- Pour yoghurt and mix well. Gently add chicken stock and remaining salt. Bring the mixture to the boil, stirring continuously. Reduce heat.
- Add drained rice, stirring occasionally till the stock reduces to the level of the rice.
- Lower heat and cook covered till the rice is tender.
- Serve hot garnished with egg, tomato, green coriander, and sprinkled with vetivier.

An All Time Favourite

This dish is a whole meal as it has mutton pieces, kidney, liver, eggs, and keema cooked over slow fire. It was one of the favourite dishes in Peshawar and an all time favourite of my grandfather's. In the Seventies, the nomenclature of this Moti Mahal pulao was changed to Gatti pulao as a tribute to one of the oldest employees of Moti Mahal, Daryaganj.

Tandoori Roti

Unleavened wholewheat flour bread

Ingredients   serves: 4

Wholewheat flour
(*atta*) ~ 1¼ cups / 225 gm
Salt ~ ½ tsp
Baking powder ~ a pinch
Cooking soda ~ a pinch
Diluted milk ~ ½-¾ cup / 100-150 ml
Dry yeast ~ ½ tsp

Method

○ Sift the wheat flour with salt, baking powder, and cooking soda.

○ Heat the diluted milk till it is lukewarm. Sprinkle yeast and mix well. Cover with a lid and keep in a warm place for 10 minutes.

○ Make a well in the centre of the flour mixture in a broad basin. Pour the yeast mixture, leave for a minute and gather the dough with the palms. (Do not knead.) Sprinkle warm water, if necessary, for mixing the dough. Keep the dough closed, so that there is enough space for the dough to rise. Leave aside for 2-3 hours.

○ Divide the dough into 4-5 balls. Roll each ball thicker than normal rotis. Sprinkle a little water over the disc and spread with hand. Heat a griddle (tawa); lay the disc flat on it so that the water applied side sticks to the pan. Cover with a lid. Cook in medium heat till the disc puffs up.

○ Turn the griddle upside down with the handle so that the other side of the disc is heated on direct flame. Carefully loosen with a flat ladle and remove from heat. Repeat with the others. Serve hot.

Rice Roti

Unleavened rice flour bread made with coconut

Ingredients   serves: 4

Rice flour (prepared from washed
and dried rice) ~ 2 cups / 230 gm
Coconut (*nariyal*),
fresh, grated ~ 2 tbsp / 8 gm
Green chillies ~ 8
Salt ~ 2 tsp / 8 gm

Green coriander (*hara dhaniya*),
chopped ~ 1 tbsp / 4 gm
Onions, finely chopped
~ ¼ cup / 30 gm
Refined oil for frying
Warm water to mix the dough

Method

○ Grind the coconut and green chillies to a fine paste and mix with
all the other ingredients except the last two. Sprinkle some warm
water and knead to a hard dough.

○ Take a thin dosa pan and pat a little dough on top making it as thin
as possible.

○ Make a few holes in the centre, add oil in and around and then
place the pan on fire. Cover the pan with a lid and cook on
medium heat carefully turning the pan for even heating.

○ When the roti becomes crisp carefully take it out from the pan. Do
not turn over. Repeat till all the dough is used up. Serve hot.

Note: Keep two such pans ready for quick serve. Wash or wipe the pan every time before
patting next ball of the dough. (Let the pan cool, and then spread the dough.)

Variations: Grated carrots along with roasted and powdered peanut or finely chopped
spring onions with stem can also be added.

Rawa Roti

Unleavened semolina bread

Ingredients   serves: 4

Semolina (*rawa*),
fine ~ 2 cups / 270 gm
Refined oil for frying
Mustard seeds (*rai*) ~ ¼ tsp
Bengal gram (*chana dal*) ~ 1 tsp
Water ~ 2 cups / 400 ml
Ground to a paste:
Green chillies ~ 8
Salt ~ 1½ tsp / 6 gm

Asafoetida (*hing*) ~ a pinch

Onions, small, chopped
~ ½ cup / 60 gm
Yoghurt (*dahi*), sour
~ 2 tbsp / 60 gm
Green coriander (*hara dhaniya*),
finely chopped ~ 1½ tbsp / 6 gm
Curry leaves (*kadhi patta*) ~ 4-5

Method

○ Heat the oil in a frying pan (deep curved); add mustard seeds
and Bengal gram. When the seeds start crackling, add water
and bring it to boil. Reduce heat, add semolina and mix by
stirring constantly.

○ Remove the pan from the heat and allow the mixture to cool.

○ Add green chilli paste, onions, yoghurt, green coriander, and curry
leaves. Knead to a thick dough.

○ Divide the dough equally into 4-5 balls. Pat the balls on a wet cloth
or polythene sheet to make thick rotis.

○ Heat a griddle (*tawa*); lay a roti flat on it and fry with enough oil
on both sides. Remove and repeat till all the rotis are fried.

Note: Use fresh not roasted semolina.

Masala Parantha

Spicy unleavened shallow-fried bread

Ingredients serves: 4

Wholewheat (*atta*) flour
~ 2 cups / 200 gm
Cumin (*jeera*) seeds, roasted,
coarsely powdered ~ ¾ tsp
Salt ~ 1 tsp / 4 gm
Red chilli powder ~ 1 tsp / 2 gm
Mango powder (*amchur*) ~ ½ tsp

Garam masala (see p. 24) ~ ½ tsp
Yoghurt (*dahi*), fresh, thick
~ ½ cup / 100 gm
Milk ~ ½ cup / 100 ml
Refined oil for
the dough ~ 5 tsp / 25 ml
Refined oil for frying

Method

○ Mix all the dry ingredients together in a mixing bowl.
○ Pour yoghurt, milk, and oil; knead to a smooth dough. Keep the dough covered for 3-4 hours.
○ Divide the dough equally into 4-5 portions. Roll each portion out into a thick disc.
○ Heat a griddle *(tawa)*; lay the disc flat on it and fry on both sides till light brown. remove and repeat till all are fried.

Naan

Light leavened bread smeared with butter

Refined flour (*maida*) ~ 5 cups / 500 gm

Salt ~ 1¼ tsp / 5 gm

Baking powder ~ ¾ tsp

Cooking soda ~ ¾ tsp

Warm milk ~ ½ cup / 100 ml

Dry yeast ~ ¾ tsp

Yoghurt (*dahi*), fresh, thick

~ ½ cup / 100 gm

Sugar ~ ½ tsp

Ghee ~ 4 tsp / 20 gm

Method

- Sift the refined flour 3 times with salt, baking powder, and cooking soda in a bowl.
- Mix the yeast granules in warm milk and keep aside for 10 minutes.
- Make a well in the centre of the flour mixture. Pour the milk mixture, yoghurt, and sugar. After a minute, add ghee and mix well.
- Gather the flour with the fingertips till it forms a soft pliable mass. Do not knead. Sprinkle some more warm water while kneading. Keep covered with enough space for the dough to raise.
- After 5-6 hours, divide the dough into even-sized balls. Roll each ball with a rolling pin into ¼"-thick disc. Pull one end to make a tear-drop shape.
- Apply water on top of the naan and turn over to a hot aluminium pan with a handle so that the water applied part sticks to the pan. Cover with a lid and allow to puff up on medium heat.
- Turn the pan upside down and cook the other side on direct flame till the top turns light golden colour.
- Serve hot with a little butter applied on top.

Aam Ki Chutney

Mango relish

Ingredients serves: 4

Mangoes, raw, peeled, and
grated to get 1 kg pulp ~ 2 kg
Ginger (*adrak*), 2" piece,
peeled, grated ~ 50 gm
Sugar ~ 7 cups / 1 kg
Salt ~ 70 gm
Garam masala (see p. 24)
~ 3-4 tsp / 6-8 gm

Red chilli powder or black
pepper (*kali mirch*) powder
~ 4 tsp / 8 gm
Acetic acid ~ 1½ tsp / 7 ml
Melon (*magaz*) seeds (optional)
~ 8 tsp / 25 gm
Sodium benzoate, dissolved in 1 tsp
hot water ~ ¼ tsp / 1 gm

Method

- Cook the mangoes and ginger together in a clean wok *(kadhai)* till the water evaporates completely.
- Add sugar and stir till it dissolves completely and the mixture thickens.
- Add salt, garam masala, red chilli or black pepper powder, and acetic acid; mix well.
- Remove the wok from the heat. Add melon seeds (optional) and mix. Add sodium benzoate and mix well.
- Cool and fill the chutney, while still warm, in a sterilized jar. Seal the jar with a lid after it cools completely.

Aloo Bhukhara Chutney

Dried plum relish

Ingredients serves: 4

Dried plums (*aloo bhukhara*),
soaked overnight in 2 cups
water in a steel bowl,
drained ~ 250 gm
Ginger (*adrak*), 1" piece ~ 1
Mint (*pudina*) leaves ~ a bunch
Sugar ~ 3 cups / 450 gm
Lemon (*nimbu*) juice
~ ¾ cup / 150 ml
Salt ~ 3 tsp / 12 gm

Green cardamom (*choti elaichi*)
seeds, powdered ~ 8-10
Black cardamom (*badi elaichi*) ~ 5-6
Black pepper (*kali mirch*)
powder ~ 1-2 tsp / 2-4 gm
Red chilli powder ~ 1 tsp / 2 gm
Raisins (*kishmish*), washed
~ 1 cup / 100 gm
Almonds (*badaam*), finely chopped
~ ¾ cup / 100 gm

Method

○ Mash and squeeze the pulp of the dried plums.

○ Grind the ginger and mint leaves together to a smooth paste.

○ To the dried plum pulp, add ginger and mint paste, sugar, and lemon juice. Cook for 5 minutes.

○ Add the salt, green cardamom powder, black cardamom, black pepper powder, red pepper powder, raisins and almonds. Cook on low heat till it thickens.

○ Remove from heat and keep aside to cool. Remove the black cardamom and fill the chutney, while still warm, in sterilized jars. Seal the jar with a lid after it cools.

Pudina Chutney

Mint relish

Ingredients serves: 4

Mint (*pudina*) leaves, washed ~ ½ cup / 7½ gm
Green coriander (*hara dhaniya*) ~ 1 cup / 25 gm
Sugar ~ 1½ cups / 225 gm
Green chillies ~ 3
Tamarind (*imli*), boiled in water ~ 2 tbsp / 12 gm
Salt ~ 1 tsp / 4 gm
Pomegranate seeds (*anar dana*) ~ 1 tsp / 3 gm
Yoghurt (*dahi*) ~ 2 cups / 400 gm

Method

○ Grind mint leaves with the other ingredients (except yoghurt) to a smooth paste.
○ Whisk yoghurt and add the ground paste to it; mix well.
○ Serve with kebabs and meals.

Khajoor-Imli Sonth

Tamarind and date chutney

Ingredients   serves: 4

Tamarind (*imli*),
deseeded ~ 1 cup / 200 gm
Jaggery (*gur*) ~ 1 cup / 200 gm
Salt ~ ¾ tsp
Black salt (*kala namak*) ~ ½ tsp
Red chilli powder ~ ¾ tsp

Dates (*khajoor*), deseeded,
cut lengthwise into 4
pieces ~ 20
Potassium meta bisulphate (KMS),
dissolved in 1 tsp hot water
~ a pinch

Method

○ Boil tamarind and jaggery in 2 cups water for 10-15 minutes on low heat. Remove and keep aside to cool.

○ Squeeze and strain the pulp. Keep aside.

○ Add salt, black salt, red chilli powder, and dates to the tamarind pulp. Cook for 5-10 minutes on low heat.

○ Keep aside to cool and then preserve in a clean bottle.

Note: If you do not want chunks of dates, deseed and boil them with tamarind and jaggery. Strain the pulp and use. If you are using *chhuaras*, soak them in water for 2 hours and then deseed and chop.

Amla Achaar

Indian gooseberry pickle

Ingredients   serves: 4

Indian gooseberries (*amla*) ~ 500 gm
Salt ~ 150 gm
Mustard (*sarson*) oil ~ ½ cup / 100 ml
Cumin (*jeera*) seeds ~ 2 tsp / 4 gm
Fennel (*moti saunf*) seeds ~ 2 tsp / 4 gm
Fenugreek seeds (*methi dana*) ~ 1-2 tsp / 3-6 gm
Red chilli powder ~ 1-2 tsp / 2-4 gm
Turmeric (*haldi*) powder ~ 1-2 tsp / 2-4 gm

Method

○ Boil Indian gooseberries in water for 5 minutes. Remove from water and mix 100 gm salt. Keep aside for 5-6 hours for the water to drain out.

○ Deseed the gooseberries and cut them into half or leave them whole.

○ Heat the oil in a wok *(kadhai)* and remove from heat. Add cumin seeds, fennel seeds, fenugreek seeds, red chilli powder, turmeric powder, and the remaining salt. Add dried plums. Cook for 1-2 minutes.

○ The pickle can be consumed the next day and not kept for more than 2 weeks.

Gajar Rai Waala

Carrot pickle flavoured with mustard

Carrots (*gajar*), peeled, cut into thin
1½"-long fingers ~ 500 gm
Salt ~ 3 tsp / 12 gm
Red chilli powder ~ 2 tsp / 4 gm
Turmeric (*haldi*) powder ~ 2 tsp / 4 gm
Mustard seeds (*rai*), powdered ~ 2 tsp / 6 gm
Vinegar (*sirka*) ~ ½ cup / 100 ml

Method

○ Add carrots to the boiling water and cook for 2 minutes.
○ Remove the carrots from water and dry them for 1-2 hours on a muslin cloth.
○ Then mix salt, red chilli powder, turmeric powder, and mustard powder with the carrots.
○ Transfer the carrot mixture to a jar. Add vinegar and shake well to mix. The pickle is ready to eat in a day.

Chatpati Hari Mirch

Green chilli pickle

Ingredients serves: 4

Green chillies, slightly thick ones, washed,
wiped dry ~ 15-20 / 200 gm
Mustard (*sarson*) powder ~ 8 tsp / 16 gm
Turmeric (*haldi*) powder ~ 1 tsp / 2 gm
Salt ~ 3 tsp / 12 gm
Mango powder (*amchur*) ~ 8 tsp / 16 gm
Refined oil ~ 5 tsp / 25 ml

Method

○ Slit the green chillies and dry in shade for 1-2 hours.
○ Mix all the dry spices together.
○ Add 1 tsp oil to the spices to bind them together.
○ Fill the prepared mixture in the green chillies.
○ Heat 4 tsp oil in a wok (*kadhai*) or a pan; add stuffed green chillies and sauté for 2-3 minutes on low heat till the chillies become slightly soft. Do not let them get discoloured.
○ Store in sterilized bottles.

Sirka Pyaz

Onions in vinegar

Ingredients serves: 4

Onions, small, peeled ~ 12-15
Salt ~ 1 tsp / 4 gm
Sugar ~ 1 tbsp / 20 gm
Beetroot (*chukander*), peeled ~ 1
White vinegar (*sirka*) ~ 1 cup / 200 ml

Method

○ Rub salt over the onions. Keep aside for half an hour.
○ Pack the onions, sugar, and beetroot in a jar. Pour the vinegar over the mixture and serve.

Variations: 1" piece ginger julienned can also be added with the onions.

Shakila Banu, the famous *qwalli* singer, performing live in Moti Mahal, Daryaganj. *Qwalli* became a staple music for Moti Mahal loyalists in the early Seventies.

Moti Mahal's *qualli* group with some of its supervisors.

Khira Dilwala Raita

Cucumber and dill in yoghurt

Ingredients serves: 4

Yoghurt (*dahi*) ~ 2½ cups / 500 gm
Cucumber (*khira*), peeled, grated ~ ½ cup
Black peppercorns (*sabut kali mirch*), ground ~ ½ tsp
Dried dill flakes ~ ½ tbsp
Sugar ~ 1 tsp / 3 gm
Salt to taste
Cumin (*jeera*) powder ~ ½ tsp

Method

○ Beat yoghurt till smooth.
○ Add all the ingredients to the yoghurt except cumin powder. Mix well.
○ Serve chilled garnished with cumin powder.

Lal Rattan Raita

Pomegranate in whisked yoghurt

Ingredients   serves: 4

Yoghurt (*dahi*) ~ 2½ cups / 500 gm
Pomegranate kernels (*anar dana*), fresh ~ 1 cup
Salt ~ 1 tsp / 4 gm
Black salt (*kala namak*) ~ ¼ tsp
Red chilli powder ~ ½ tsp
Cumin (*jeera*) seeds, roasted, ground ~ 1 tsp / 2 gm
Pineapple (*ananas*), tinned ~ 2 pieces
Green coriander (*hara dhaniya*), chopped ~ 1 tbsp / 4 gm

Method

○ Beat the yoghurt till smooth. Add pomegranate kernels, salt, black salt, red chilli powder, and cumin powder; mix well. Transfer into a serving dish.

○ Surround the dish with pineapple rings. Serve garnished with few pomegranate kernels and green coriander.

Khira Moong Dal Salad

Cucumber and green gram salad

Ingredients serves: 4

Cucumber (*khira*), thin, tender,
scrape outer skin, check for
bitterness and then slice into thin
rounds, shred the rounds again
into 1½"-thin pieces ~ 3-4
Green gram (*moong dal*)
~ 1½ tbsp / 27 gm
Green coriander (*hara dhaniya*),
finely chopped ~ 1 tbsp / 4 gm

Salt to taste
Coconut (*nariyal*), fresh, grated
~ 1 tbsp / 4 gm
Dry red chillies (*sookhi lal mirch*),
cooked in 2-3 tbsp yoghurt for 2-3
minutes ~ 3-4
Juice of lemon (*nimbu*) ~ 1
Refined oil ~ 1 tsp / 5 ml
Mustard seeds (*rai*) ~ ¼ tsp

Method

○ Boil the green gram in water till they split. Drain excess water.
○ Mix the cucumber, boiled green gram, green coriander, salt, coconut, and fried red chillies in a bowl. Add lemon juice; toss well
○ Heat the oil in a pan; add mustard seeds. When they start spluttering, remove and add to the salad. Mix well.
○ Serve within 10 minutes.

Note: When salt is added to the cucumber, the mixture becomes soggy.

Variations: Use sprouted green gram (raw) instead of cooked green gram. Raw cabbage shredded finely can also be mixed with green gram to make salad. Use green chillies instead of fried red chillies. (Make into paste and fry in oil along with mustard.)

Fruit Salad

Ingredients serves: 4

Bananas (*kela*), ripe, peeled, diced into cubes ~ 3
Apple (*seb*), peeled, diced ~ 1
Lemon (*nimbu*) ~ 1
Oranges (*santra*), peeled, diced ~ 2
Green grapes (*angoor*) ~ 1 small bunch
Mango (*aam*), ripe ~ 1
Pomegranate seeds (*anar dana*), fresh ~ 2 tbsp
Pineapple (*ananas*) ~ ½
Candied cherries ~ a few
Raisins (*kishmish*), optional ~ a few
Sugar ~ ½ -¾ cup / 75-112 gm

Method

○ Mix all the fruits together in a bowl.
○ Melt the sugar in a pan over low heat with very little water till half of it melts. Mix it with the prepared fruits.
○ Chill and then serve.

Note: Mix the lemon juice with the apples and bananas immediately after cutting to prevent it from turning brown. Chop with a stainless steel knife.

DESSERTS

Kesar Pista Kulfi

Homemade ice cream with saffron and pistachios

Ingredients serves: 4

Milk, full cream ~ 20 cups / 4 lt
Sugar ~ 2 cups / 300 gm
Saffron (*kesar*) ~ a few strands
Pistachios (*pista*) ~ ½ cup / 100 gm
Green cardamom (*choti elaichi*) powder ~ ²/₃ tsp / 2 gm
Rose water (*gulab jal*) ~ 2-3 drops

Method

○ Boil milk over medium heat till it is reduced to half its quantity and is of a thick, yellowish consistency.

○ Gradually, add sugar and cook for another 5 minutes. Add saffron strands and mix well. Remove from heat, cool and add pistachios and green cardamom powder; mix well.

○ Fill the mixture in conical plastic or aluminium-*kulfi* moulds. Seal tightly with silver foil and freeze for 2 hours. Shake the mould 2 times during the first hour of freezing to avoid crystallization.

○ Remove the moulds from the freezer, dip the bottom of the moulds in hot water just for a few seconds to loosen the sides, and invert on to the serving dish.

○ Serve chilled sprinkled with a few drops of rose water.

Mango Kulfi

Homemade mango ice cream

Ingredients serves: 4

Mango pulp ~ 2½ cups / 500 gm
Milk, full cream ~ 5 cups / 1 lt
Sugar ~ 3 tbsp / 60 gm
Saffron (*kesar*) ~ a few strands
Cream, double ~ ¾ cup / 150 gm
Pistachios (*pista*) ~ 1 tbsp / 15 gm
Rose water (*gulab jal*)~ 1 tsp / 5 ml

Method

○ Boil the milk in a heavy-bottomed pan; lower heat and simmer. Add sugar and cook on low heat till the milk thickens and is reduced to one third.

○ Add mango pulp and saffron and cook for 3-4 minutes on low heat, stirring constantly. Remove and cool at room temperature. Mix in the cream.

○ Pour the mixture in individual kulfi moulds; seal tightly with silver foil and freeze for 5 hours, at least. During the first hour of freezing shake the moulds at least 4 times to avoid crystallization.

○ Remove the moulds from the freezer, dip the bottom of the moulds in hot water just for a few seconds to loosen the sides, and invert on to serving dishes.

○ Serve chilled garnished with pistachios and sprinkled with rose water.

Phirni

Rice pudding flavoured with pistachios

Ingredients serves: 4

Milk, full cream ~ 5 cups / 1 lt
Rice flour ~ ½ cup / 57 gm
Sugar ~ 1 cup / 150 gm
Rose water (*gulab jal*) ~ 5 drops
Green cardamom (*choti elaichi*) powder ~ ²/₃ tsp / 3 gm
Saffron (*kesar*) ~ ¼ tsp
Pistachios (*pista*) ~ ¼ cup / 50 gm

Method

○ Heat half the quantity of milk in a heavy-bottomed pan and bring to the boil.

○ Dissolve the rice flour in the remaining milk and slowly add to the hot milk, in the pan, on low heat, stirring constantly, until the mixture becomes thick (like custard).

○ Add sugar and cook for 2-3 minutes. Remove and keep aside to cool. Add rose water and green cardamom powder.

○ Pour in individuals bowls and garnish with saffron and pistachios.

Shahi Tukra

Deep-fried bread topped with thickened milk

Ingredients serves: 4

White bread, cut into ¾" pieces,
crust removed ~ 10 slices
Ghee ~ ¾ cup / 150 gm
For the sugar syrup:
Sugar ~ 4 tbsp / 60 gm
Water ~ 1 cup / 200 ml
Rose water (*gulab jal*) ~ 5 drops

Milk, full cream
~ 5 cups / 1 lt
Sugar ~ 2 cups / 300 gm
Pistachios (*pista*), chopped
~ 5 tsp / 25 gm
Saffron (*kesar*), dissolved in 1 tbsp
warm milk ~ ¼ tsp

Method

○ Fry the bread pieces in ghee till golden brown.

○ For the sugar syrup, mix sugar with water and boil till the water is reduced to half. Keep aside to cool. Then add rose water. Soak the fried slices in the sugar syrup.

○ Boil the milk in a heavy-bottomed pot. Simmer for about 30 minutes or until it thickens. Gradually mix in the sugar and stir for 3-4 minutes or till the sugar dissolves completely. Cool and chill.

○ Arrange the slices on a dish and pour the thickened milk over it. Refrigerate for some time.

○ Serve chilled garnished with pistachios and saffron.

Badaam Halwa

Almond pudding

Ingredients serves: 4

Almonds (*badaam*), blanched in hot water
for 1 hour ~ 2½ cups / 500 gm
Ghee ~ 1 cup / 200 gm
Milk ~ 1 cup / 200 ml
Sugar ~ 2 cups / 300 gm
Saffron (*kesar*) ~ a few strands
Green cardamom (*choti elaichi*) powder ~ 1½ tsp / 3 gm
Silver leaves (*varq*) ~ 2

Method

- Remove the outer skin of the almonds and grind to a smooth paste with a little milk.
- Heat the ghee in a heavy-based pan; add almond paste and sauté over medium heat till the mixture becomes golden brown.
- Add milk and sugar and cook for 10-12 minutes over medium heat, until the mixture becomes thick.
- Remove the pan from the heat; add saffron and green cardamom powder. Spread the mixture over a greased tray. Cut into small triangles, put silver leaves over it and serve chilled.

Glossary of Food and Cooking Terms

Batter: A mixture of flour, liquid and sometimes other ingredients of a thin, creamy consistency.

Blend: To mix together thoroughly two or more ingredients.

Broil: Dry roast the food items in a heavy-bottomed pan over low heat without using oil or water.

Coat: To cover food that is to be fried with flour, egg and breadcrumbs or batter.

Curdle: To separate milk into curd and whey by acid or excessive heat.

Dough: A thick mixture of uncooked flour and liquid, often combined with other ingredients: the mixture can be handled as a solid mass.

Fry: To cook in hot fat or oil. In the case of shallow-frying only a small quantity of fat is used in a shallow pan. The food must be turned halfway through to cook both sides. In the case of deep-frying, sufficient fat is used to cover the food completely.

Garnish: An edible decoration added to a savoury or sweet dish to improve its appearance.

Grease: To coat the surface of a dish or tin with fat to prevent food from sticking to it.

Grind: To reduce hard food such as pulses, lentils, rice, and so forth, to fine or coarse paste in a grinder or blender.

Julienne: Garnished with fine strips of cooked or raw vegetables.

Knead: To work a dough by hand or machine until smooth.

Marinade: A seasoned mixture of oil, vinegar, lemon juice, and so forth, in which meat, poultry or fish is left for some time to soften and add flavour to it.

Patty: A small individual pie.

Purée: To press food through a fine sieve or blend it in a blender or food processor to a smooth, thick mixture.

Rub in: To incorporate the ingredients using the fingertips.

Sauté: To cook in an open pan in hot, shallow fat, tossing the food to prevent it from sticking.

Seasoning: Salt, pepper, spices, herbs, and so forth, added to give depth of flavour.

Sift: To shake a dry ingredient through a sieve or flour sifter, to remove lumps.

Simmer: To boil gently on low heat.

Skewer: Fasten together pieces of food compactly on a specially designed long pin, for cooking.

Steam: To cook food in steam. Generally food to be steamed is put in a perforated container which is placed above a pan of boiling water. The food should not come into contact with the water.

Stir: To mix with a circular action, usually with a spoon, fork or spatula.

Syrup: A concentrated solution of sugar in water.

Whip: To beat rapidly and introduce air into an ingredient; usually cream.

Whisk: To beat rapidly to introduce air into a light mixture; usually of egg.

Index

Murgh Pakora 37
Murgh Tikka Masala 38
Reshmi Kebab 52
Saag Murgh 40
Tandoori Batyer 54
Tandoori Murgh 34

Lamb

Badaam Parsinda Gosht 67
Boti Kebabs 59
Barra Kebabs 66
Chaamp 55
Gosht Dopiazza 62
Gosht Passanda 57
Gosht Shahi Korma 58
Khatta Gosht 56
Nihari Gosht 60
Seekh Kebabs 65
Shammi Kebabs 63

Fish and Other Seafoods

Fish Kebabs 69
Fish Tikka 70
Khatti Machchi 71
Machchi Punjabi Curry 72
Sharabi Jhinga 73
Tamatar Jhinga 74

VEGETARIAN

Bharwan Dum Aloo 86
Dal Makhani 88
Jimikand Ke Kebabs 79
Kadhai Khumb 84
Kadhai Paneer 85
Mirchi Ka Salan 82
Navrattan Korma 89
Paneer Ke Kebabs 81
Seekh-e-Subz 80
Tandoori Aloo 78
Tandoori Arbi 77
Tandoori Gobi 76
Tandoori Vegetables 83

ACCOMPANIMENTS
Rice

Gosht Biryani 96
Gatti Pulao 98
Murgh Biryani 94
Subz Pulao 92

Breads

Masala Parantha 103
Naan 104
Rawa Roti 102

Rice Roti 101
Tandoori Roti 100

Chutneys, Pickles and Salads

Aam Ki Chutney 105
Aloo Bhukhara Chutney 106
Amla Achaar 109
Chatpati Hari Mirch 111
Gajar Rai Waala 110
Khajoor-Imli Sonth 108
Khira Dilwala Raita 113
Lal Rattan Raita 114
Pudina Chutney 107
Sirka Pyaz 112
Fruit Salad 116
Khira Moong Dal Salad 115

DESSERTS

Kesar Pista Kulfi 118
Mango Kulfi 119
Phirni 120
Shahi Tukra 121